W9-DFQ-284

GAMES, ANYONE?

GAMES, ANYONE?

A Witty Collection of Adult Games

by

ROBERT THOMSEN

1964

DOUBLEDAY & COMPANY, INC.

GARDEN CITY, NEW YORK

FIRST EDITION

Library of Congress Catalog Card Number 64-19251
Copyright © 1964 by Robert Thomsen
All Rights Reserved
Printed in the United States of America

Contents

GAMES, ANYONE?

1: Game People

I have a brother who believes—quite seriously—that our world is divided evenly between adventurous liberals and timid conservatives. Liberals, of course, will gladly risk everything to break through into the next dimension, while the conservatives, at any cost, want to hang on to the status quo.

S. N. Behrman sees another grouping. In one of his early plays he insists the two kinds of people in life are "those whom one keeps waiting and those for whom one waits." And Daniel George has reached the conclusion not so much that we are leaders or the led, but that we are all either preachers or preached-at. In Baltimore a niece of mine has simplified it even more. To her, we are cat people or dog people.

This could be. I know that in my early days I was able to classify along with the best of them. (Does anyone remember extroverts and introverts?) But I am afraid experience, whereas it may not teach you anything, does have a way of playing hell with easy labels. The preached-at I find beginning to preach, the led wander off on their own, and certainly the ones I kept waiting yesterday I am waiting for today.

For me now there is only one true category. Always, irrefutably my world's been divided into game people and non-game people. And knowing this, I also know now there is nothing to be done about it, the gap is there, and God be with the host who tries to mingle us.

Actually I had no choice. Born the youngest son of a youngest son—back four generations to my certain knowledge —all of us have been incorrigible game-lovers. Let a Thomsen

go anywhere, let him stand before the full majesty of the
Grand Canyon, like as not he'll ask you for the name of a
movie star with the same initials.

(*Note:* Gary Cooper, Gower Champion, Gladys Cooper
. . . any G. C. will satisfy us.)

My poor father—he was the greatest, an addict's addict.
Late in life he managed one trip to Europe and I was taken
along as his partner, his foil. I can see him now on a hot July
afternoon—he'd wandered off from the other members of our
Cook's tour and stood alone in the center of the Place de la
Concorde—staring up at the Eiffel Tower. For a long time
he did not speak, then he smiled sweetly, his whole being
relaxed. "Ernie Truex," he said.

Dear Pops. One of my private games is wondering where
you are now, and wondering if you mind being a full three
thirds of a ghost.

Perhaps a word of warning should come here. If this sort
of thing means nothing to you, if by some unhappy chance
you are not a game man, do yourself a favor, stop now. For
there is no way to explain this mania, just as we who are
afflicted know there is no known cure for us. We can only
share our experiences one with the other and hope that along
the way we'll run into more of our kind.

This book then is dedicated to my fellow game addicts.

As for you others, take it back immediately, try for an
exchange now before you muck up the following pages with
your dirty, ungamely paws, before you go a little mad trying
to figure out our strange, inexplicable obsession, which I am
sure none of us would surrender, even if the doctors came
up with a cure. It is our cross and we love it.

2: *Reversals*

To begin with a few games you may not know.

Later there will be time for old standbys, chatty prose about origins, historical backgrounds, suggestions for cheating, etc. . . . but now to work.

Take a blank piece of paper, a large one. (Pads of legal ruled paper are basic equipment for game buffs.)

Down the left-hand side write the alphabet in a column with a separate line for each letter, all the way from A to Z.

This one can be played in various ways, alone, with another player, or even in large—if compatible—groups. You should be warned, if played alone it can become habit-forming. But however many you may be, you start off with the alphabet down the left-hand column.

Next, on the top line, opposite the letter A, write the name of a famous person whose *first* name begins with A (Alfred Knopf). Then opposite the letter B, someone whose first name begins with B (Barbara Hutton). Opposite C a famous first named C, and so on down through Z.

(X will give you pause, but carry on, there's always Xavier Cugat, and you'll think of others.)

When your list is complete, if you are playing with another, exchange papers. If there is a larger group, pass the lists around in any manner you choose. If alone, just be brave. After all, you are challenging yourself.

Next, in another column at the right-hand side of the paper you have just received, begin a second list, *reversing the initials of the names found in column one* (opposite Alfred Knopf you must give a K. A.—Konrad Adenauer).

Next reverse the initials you find on the second line (Barbara Hutton—Harry Belafonte), and so on, until the column is completed or someone gives up.

Example lists appear on the following pages.

It is wise to set a time limit before you start. Ten minutes may be too strict, but a half hour is surely wildly indulgent.

Also you should decide who is acceptable. I am a purist here. For example, Senator Goldwater I would never allow as S. G. He is Barry Goldwater, as clear a B. G. as I know. The same goes for Pope Paul as a P. P. or King Alphonse as a K. A. I also take a very dim view of trying to pass off Aunt Bessie no matter how famous she is to you. She has a last name. She is not an A. B.

Perhaps you should be a little lenient the first time through. After all we can't be sure whom we're up against at some parties and there is no point in alienating nongame people too early. Their true colors will come out soon enough.

There are variations of Reversals but none have improved on the simple form of the original. Some men derive a certain monotonous pleasure from going through the alphabet without reversing the initials. Apparently they are quite content to make lists changing *only* the first letter (Anne Andrews, Bud Abbott, Charles Addams, Dana Andrews, Edward Albee . . . and on and on). Then I'm told they do the same thing with B (Alice Brady, Buddy Baer, Cartier-Bresson). Well, it's their way. Live and let live.

Leonard Spigelgass, the author of *A Majority of One* and some three thousand screenplays, is indeed a funny man as well as one of the last writers alive to be concerned with the old-fashioned "well-made play." His are comedies where characters enter, usually through doors, meet one another, face a situation, and at the end of three regulation acts reach a solution. He writes plots which, someone has pointed out, always have a beginning, a muddle, and an end.

A good man to have about. And of course he's an ardent game-player. My only quarrel with Leonard is about rules. He accepts not only famous names, but also *any* name, or *any phrase* that is well known or forever joined. (He will use dull thud for a D. T. and for a C. B. he'll allow Call Bureau.) This is more than permissive, it is subversive.

Be sure to settle your rules before you begin.

About that warning mentioned above—the real addict has undoubtedly already sensed the danger, felt the compulsion beginning to take over; he knows that from here in, any initial anywhere must be filled out, and initials are everywhere.

I find this is especially insidious for those who live in states that print letters on license plates. Connecticut, which often uses *only* letters, could secede from the Union tomorrow, and I, for one, would not lift a hand to stop it. But New York is beginning to have its share.

Only last month at the corner of Park and Seventy-first Street I spotted a New York plate with no number, but three very distinct initials, J.C.S.

How could I go on? The car—it was a Rolls—was waiting for a light. I remember standing on the corner staring at it and realizing that no other thought could enter my mind till I filled that one out. And it happened. In a flash. Of course! Joan Crawford Steele.

I admit I was proud. I looked up and beamed and I found that I was looking . . . yes, you've guessed it, I was looking into those fabulous eyes-Benedict of the one and only Mrs. Joan Crawford Steele, who sat on the back seat. And she smiled back at me.

P. S.: This may not be your game at all. You may never feel the need to fill in initials. If not, and you find yourself surrounded by filler-inners, you'll probably understand Beatrice Lillie's feeling when she first saw television. (And for my money this remains the most intelligent comment ever made about the magic box.) It was back in 1949 and after she had watched her first show, someone asked what she thought. Miss Lillie came straight to the point. "Television," she said, "will cause a lot of drinking in the home."

EXAMPLE:

A	Adlai Stevenson	Sherman Adams
B	Buster Crabbe	Cecil Beaton
C	Charles Addams	Al Capone
D	Dore Schary	Shelagh Delaney
E	Edward Albee	Albert Einstein
F	Frances Perkins	Pierre Fresnay
G	Garson Kanin	Kate Greenaway
H	Henry Luce	Lorraine Hansberry
I	Ian Fleming	Frieda Inescort
J	John Steinbeck	Salome Jens
K	Knute Rockne	Ronald Knox
L	Lyndon Johnson	Jack Lemmon
M	Margaret Sanger	Sal Mineo
N	Nelson Rockefeller	Richard Nixon
O	Orville Prescott	Peter O'Toole
P	Pierre Salinger	Sidney Poitier
Q	Quentin Roosevelt	Richard Quine
R	Richard Burton	Bobo Rockefeller
S	Stan Musial	Menasha Skulnik
T	Thomas Wolfe	William Tilden
U	Ursula Parrott	Peter Ustinov
V	Vivien Leigh	Lupe Velez
W	Winthrop Ames	Audrey Wood
X	Xavier Cugat	Christian Xervos
Y	Yul Brynner	Blanche Yurka
Z	* Zachary Scott	Sam Zimbalist

* Spend every free moment thinking up Z's. Here are a few that reverse nicely: Zero Mostel and Maurice Zolotow, Fred Zinnemann, and Zelda Fitzgerald, Zasu Pitts and Peter Zinberg—a psychiatrist, honestly; I know some of his patients.

ALLITERATION—For Postgraduates only.

A	Adele Astaire	Abigail Adams
B	Bernard Baruch	Bertolt Brecht
C	Cassius Clay	Cheryl Crawford
D	David Dubinsky	Deanna Durbin
E	Edith Evans	Edward Everett
F	Frank Fay	Fred Finkelhoff
G	Greta Garbo	George Gershwin
H	Helen Hayes	Helen Hokinson
I		
J	Jesse James	Joe Jackson
K	Kurt Kasznar	Kay Kyser
L	Leonard Lyons	Lawrence Langner
M	Mickey Mantle	Marya Mannes
N	Nita Naldi	Nancy Nolan
O	Ole Olson	Oliver Onions
P	Pablo Picasso	Patti Page
Q		
R	Richard Rovere	Robert Ryan
S	Stuart Symington	Simone Signoret
T	Tom Tryon	Terry-Thomas
U		
V	Vivian Vance	
W	Woodrow Wilson	Walter Winchell
X		
Y		
Z		

NOTE: I leave the blanks for you to fill in.

VERY SPECIAL: Down the far left-hand side write the alphabet in its proper order (A to Z), then in another column beside it reverse the alphabet (Z to A), and try to fill it in. Here's an example, but do your own first.

A	Z	Adolph Zukor
B	Y	Brigham Young
C	X	Christian Xervos
D	W	David Wayne
E	V	Erich Von Stroheim
F	U	*
G	T	Gene Tunney
H	S	Harriet Beecher Stowe
I	R	Irene Rich
J	Q	José Quintero
K	P	Katherine Anne Porter
L	O	Laurence Olivier
M	N	Mabel Normand
N	M	Norman Mailer
O	L	Oscar Levant
P	K	Percy Kilbride (Pa Kettle)
Q	J	*
R	I	Robert Ingersoll
S	H	Sonja Henie
T	G	Thomas Gainsborough
U	F	*
V	E	Vince Edwards
W	D	Walter Damrosch
X	C	Xavier Cugat
Y	B	Yogi Berra
Z	A	Zoë Akins

* Again the blanks are for your delectation.

To get warmed up, practice on this:

A	
B	
C	
D	
E	
F	
G	
H	
I	
J	
K	
L	
M	
N	
O	
P	
Q	
R	
S	
T	
U	
V	
W	
X	
Y	
Z	

A	
B	
C	
D	
E	
F	
G	
H	
I	
J	
K	
L	
M	
N	
O	
P	
Q	
R	
S	
T	
U	
V	
W	
X	
Y	
Z	

3: Play Titles

Very few people, I am sure, have grown up in these United States without at some time or other playing Geography. It's a perfectly sensible game, may even be educational for the young, but after a time it begins to pall.

Play Titles, on the other hand, which must be an outgrowth of Geography, stands up. (I believe it began when our theater was in a much healthier state and touring companies spread out across the nation. I know I was introduced to it when I was connected with a very unsound stock company in the early thirties. We did split weeks, two nights on Nantucket Island and four nights in West Falmouth. There was only one way to make the jump, by boat. The full company would stretch out on the top deck, and knowing we had uninterrupted hours before us, we'd play endless rounds of Play Titles. Basking in the breeze, sailing out of old Woods Hole . . .)

The rules and the scoring are exactly those of Geography, and any number may join in.

One player starts off, but instead of giving the name of a river or a mountain or town, he calls out the title of a play (for example, *Who's Afraid of Virginia Woolf?*).

The game moves clockwise. The player on his left has been given an F (since Woolf ends in F) and he now must think of a play beginning with F (*Funny Thing Happened on the Way to the Forum**).

* Someone may challenge this, saying it's "A Funny Thing Happened . . .". Don't let it throw you, there are lots of F's: *Fanny, Fanny's First Play, First Year, Funny Girl*, etc. *The* at the beginning of a title may present a problem too, so again it is well to decide on rules before you start to play.

The one on his left must now come up with an M (*Mary, Mary*). And he must do this quickly before some impatient member of the company begins counting, slowly, one . . . two . . . three . . . At the count of ten, if he is still floundering he is declared a third of a ghost and the problem passes on to the player at his left.

A third of a ghost may continue to play, of course, until he has fumbled twice more, at which time he becomes three thirds of a ghost.

Attitudes vary as to what should be the fate of a full ghost. Many hold that he is out of the game and declared one of the losers. But there are those who believe he may hang around and try to get other players to speak to him. If he is successful (usually by tricky personal questions, unrelated to the serious business of the game), then the player who has spoken to the ghost is himself contaminated and becomes immediately a full ghost and is dropped from the game. Presumably he, too, may now try to seduce those still playing into speaking to him. And so it goes, an ever-narrowing circle, the winner being the one who has managed to think up a title each time his turn has arrived and has successfully resisted answering the ghosts.

If you think I changed the subject back there when someone was stuck with a Y (*Mary, Mary*), you're right. Y's are hell, but here are a few: *Yeomen of the Guard, You Can't Take It with You, Young Woodley,* and *Yellow Jack.*

You also might do some research on E's. It's amazing the number of plays that end in E; very few, however, begin with it. Hoard E's. (*East Lynne, Elizabeth the Queen, Enter Laughing, Edward, My Son*)

P.S. If you are one of those who must win at any cost, the Samuel French catalogue is your book. Also a quick glance at the index of *The Best Plays of the Year* just before the game should make you shine.

Variations: The most obvious variation, of course, is Movie Titles, but if you are past forty don't think of playing this with anyone fourteen to eighteen. The number of pictures they have seen and remember is staggering.

Song Titles is another version, and Titles of Novels will serve for a round or two in some circles, but I find it difficult to challenge the title of a novel. How can you prove there has been no book called *Troubled Summer* or *Love Lingers On?*

4: Shedding Light

Divorce proceedings have been instigated—and in a few Western states substantial sums of alimony awarded—on the grounds of the mental cruelty displayed while playing this little number.

One person leads off by describing or "shedding light"

about a character. The character may be either living or dead, dealer's choice.

The facts mentioned—as well as the language used—are usually as obscure as possible. Indeed, obscurity is the point and purpose of the game: to go on as long as you can without letting your opponent(s) know who you are talking about.

For some unknown reason this game is always played in the first person.

Example:

"I was born in a Southern clime . . . the youngest of seven children. . . . One of my brothers became world famous in his chosen field, but at the time of my death everyone in my country knew my name. . . ."

If no one shows any signs of catching on, the Lead-off must continue.

"I was called mad, the most loathsome criminal of the century . . . yet I claimed I was a patriot and believed history would honor me. . . . When I committed my heinous crime a few men thought they heard me say that I was sick, but in truth I was quoting the noble Brutus, '*Sic semper tyrannis.*' . . ."

At this point some bright soul will undoubtedly catch on, but instead of screaming out the name and thus ending the game, with great self-control he will ask one of those obscure questions such as, "Does your first name end with the letter N?" And since the Lead-off knows he has been talking about John Wilkes Booth, he'll have to say yes, and from here on the two of them, the Lead-off and the bright soul, team up and continue shedding light together.

"For weeks after I committed my crime the nation mourned the man I'd murdered. . . ."

Still no response? On it goes.

"I was hunted down through Maryland . . . into Virginia . . . hiding in barns by day, moving on at night . . . suffering from a leg injury I had sustained when my boot caught in an American flag. . . . Finally I was captured and shot to death in a tobacco shed. . . . It was on an April night in the year 1865."

At this point, if anyone is still out, the Lead-off has a choice. He may narrow his eyes and announce that the American flag draped a box at Ford's Theatre in which Abraham Lincoln sat. He can do this, or he can decide to go on shedding light for the rest of the night.

This, of course, is an ideal sport for biography readers. If you can choose a character who has been the subject of a tome you've just read (and you are sure no one else in the group has read it) your chances of being the center of attention are limitless. Or if you have total recall of gossip, this one was made for you.

A word of warning about choosing a friend as your subject: Once in New Canaan, Connecticut, I watched what had started off as a happy weekend, fall to pieces, with cars heading back to the city early Sunday morning—all because I had chosen to shed some light about a very nice girl named Jan.

Jan is an actress and, poor dear, in the last few years she has been cast in a few pretty seedy roles. Carried away with the possibilities here, I began obscurely, indirectly, hinting at some of the things I had seen her do on the stage. "I was involved," I said, "in a situation where I made love to a plainclothesman, and later found two dollars pinned to my pillow. . . ."

This met an icy silence. It meant nothing to anyone. Apparently they had not seen the play, so I shifted to real life. (And right here was my mistake. I should have stuck with the roles she played on stage, or with her real life offstage.)

"I was married to the same man three times," I said. And this was quite true. First, Jan had been married by a justice of the peace, then she became a convert and a second ceremony was arranged with the blessing—or the partial bless-

ing—of the Church. In time her husband, the same man—
there was no shifting around here—became a Roman Catholic
and a third gala ceremony was performed with the priest
happily blessing both sides.

A perfectly true, and to me reasonable, series of events,
but no one except me had known about them. And as I went
on shedding more light, becoming more and more obvious,
and as others began catching on, tempers began rising.

Several hours and many martinis later, I was being accused of the most outrageous things, such as deliberately trying to ruin poor Jan's reputation. No one remembered that
I had said she had played certain low-life roles on stage. Oh
no, I'd said she was a tramp. What about that incident where
two dollars had been left on her pillow?

Far, far safer to choose someone you know to be dead,
someone whose moral reputation has been established be-
yond bickering. And forget about actresses on or off stage.

It can be a good game. Try it. Just be sure when you've caught on and recognize who is being described, to indicate this with a most indirect question. Only the Lead-off should know whom you have in mind. From here in, the two of you will continue—happily we hope—shedding your light together.

5:   *Revelations*

Remember *Rashomon*, the Japanese film where the events of a crime were related differently by the characters involved? This form of storytelling has always fascinated me. I first became aware of its possibilities when I was a boy in Baltimore. I knew an old lawyer then whose practice was primarily divorce cases. Through the years Mr. Smithers—I think that was his name—had compiled a list of questions which he put to young couples who came to him for a divorce. The one question on his list that has stayed with me was the one in which he asked the husbands and wives to write down the most meaningful events of their marriage.

Out of twenty-five couples—that is to say, out of fifty persons interrogated—he seldom found more than three identical answers. This never ceased to baffle old Smithers.

I sometimes wonder if he would have been equally baffled by the scorepads in a game of *Revelations*. In the last few years I have been playing it with husbands and wives, brothers and sisters, room-mates, business partners, fathers, sons, and rarely has anyone been able to identify his closest companion in more than three out of ten answers.

Unlike most games, this one works only with groups who know each other, or think they know each other pretty well. Also there are two special requirements for *Revelations:* a little time is needed for preparation, and one must have a genuine desire to be honest with oneself. If that hasn't scared you off, here's how it goes.

A list of sixteen questions is given out in advance. If it's a weekend party, several hours before game time should be ample. If you are gathering for an evening, mail the questions out the day before you plan to meet. A set of instructions should accompany each list. The following is a sample which you may wish to paraphrase, but these points in general should be covered:

Rules — Suggestions — Helpful Hints

1. *All* questions must be answered.

2. In questions requiring a name in the answer, the name of any person living or dead may be used, *except the name of someone you know will be present when the answers are read.*

3. Questions are to be discussed with no one except _____ _____ (name of host) who will be available at _____ (give address) or by phone be-

tween the hours of ————————————————
(give time and phone number).

With these instructions, deliver to each player one set of the following questions.

REVELATIONS

1. If it were necessary to spend five thousand dollars on myself within the next thirty minutes (no gifts for others may be included in the answer) I should like to be in ——————————

————(name of shop, city or country).

2. I must spend the next two months shut up in a two-bed hospital room. I am not ill, I'm in no pain, but I cannot get out of bed. I will have no visitors during this period, and aside from impersonal hospital attendants I shall speak to no one except the patient in the next bed. In this situation I should like the patient to be—————————————————————

—————————————(name of patient, male or female).

3. It is within my power to perform one good deed for the human race. This power includes all of the supernatural black magic of the past and all of the yet undiscovered scientific power of the future. There is only one condition: if I perform this deed, I will receive no publicity for it. In fact, no one will ever know that I was connected with it. Under these circumstances I should like to ————————————————————————————————.

4. I may have cocktails every day next week with anyone I choose. Here is my list: ————————————————————————————(living or dead).

5. As I face the next twelve months (quite seriously now) my greatest fear for myself is ————————————————————————.

6. As I face the next twelve months my greatest fear for the world is _____

_____

_____ .

7. The time I remember laughing hardest in my life was _____

_____

_____ (give name of play, book, movie, etc. If it was an occasion which you shared with someone who will be present at the party, try to describe it without giving your identity away).

8. Tomorrow morning (take this one slowly) I shall awaken as someone else. (The only alternative you are given is that you do not awaken at all.) Under these circumstances I should like to awaken as:

A. _____

B. _____ .

9. Tomorrow morning's paper will carry the announcement of the death of a prominent American citizen. I should feel the greatest personal loss if this were the announcement of the death of

_____

_____ .

10. Tonight I may wear any piece of wardrobe ever designed. I have no fear of the law, or of the comments of my friends. In this situation I should like to wear _____

_____

_____

_____ .

11. I have a son twenty-four years old, an intelligent, healthy young man, who has spent a year in New York and a year in Europe. He comes home to tell me that he has decided to become a Trappist monk. At hearing this news I would:
(Check one of the following)

A. Accept his decision.

B. Accept his decision happily.

C. Try to dissuade him.

D. Kill him.

E. Kill myself.

12. If your answer to Question 11 is C, state briefly what you feel your strongest argument would be: _____
_____
_____.

13. Each man and each woman has one quality of which he or she is justly proud. Quite honestly I am proud of the following quality in myself: _____
_____
_____.

14. Most of us are agreed that the world would be a better place with more beautiful, intelligent people. To help bring this happy state about, I should like the following persons to reproduce:
_____ and _____
_____ and _____
_____ and _____
_____ and _____

15. As in Question 3 you had the power to do one good deed, so now you may commit one murder, and no one will ever know about it. You can rid the world of one person and never get blamed. Who? _____
_____.

16. Now that this party is almost over, the thing I am looking forward to most is _____
_____.

When the players assemble, all answers are collected and each sheet is marked with a letter (A, B, C, D, etc.).

Scorepads are then given out with the names of the players written across the top, and down the left-hand side of the pads there should be a column of numbers 1 to 16.

As the host starts reading aloud, your job is to figure out which player gave which answers. There are two ways of doing this. First, the host may read aloud all of the answers on Sheet A and you can mark an A under the name of the player whose answers you think are being read.

A more amusing way I find is to have all of the answers to Question 1 read together, then after reviewing the lot, you mark under each player's name the Sheet letter you think belongs to him.

When all answers have been read and all scorepads filled in, the host reveals whose name appears on each sheet.

Earlier I suggested that this was fine for weekends, but to me it is the perfect holiday game. What is better for that long stretch of Christmas Day? After the dinner's been eaten, the packages all opened and the presents admired—what do you do? Also there's a fair chance that you're spending Christmas with a group you at least think you know.

Perhaps I feel so strongly about this because I first played it on a Christmas evening at Katherine and Dale Eunson's.

Katherine Eunson is a remarkable person for many reasons —a good writer, a devout movie fan (and how many of those are around now?)—but above all she is the most ardent and tireless game girl I ever met. In the first place, she has total recall for the nonessential and that I am convinced is the real secret. I know I will never forget an afternoon when she won ten dollars from me being Someone Beginning with N. After three hours of questioning, I finally got her to admit that she was Nibbles. And Nibbles, in case you have forgotten, was the hero of a book by Elizabeth Taylor. (That's right, Cleopatra Elizabeth Taylor.) Miss Taylor wrote a whole book about her pet chipmunk when she was twelve. M-G-M saw that it was published and of course Katherine read it and remembered.

She (Katherine) is very talented, she has added many questions to Revelations, and that after all is part of the game. I'm sure you will think up some of your own. If you want to be more personal than those listed here, try it.

However it's played, I can guarantee you'll be stumped somewhere along the line trying to figure who gave which answer.

6: *Someone Beginning with B*

Once in Beverly Hills I was closeted in an elevator with two physicians. I knew who they were, but we didn't speak; they appeared to be in deep consultation.

"I always use ice," the first one said.

"And I always use heat," the second said.

"Ice." The first was insistent.

"No, deep heat." Then as the car stopped and I followed them off, they were silent, both lost in thought.

At the front door, the first one shook his head. "Ice," he said. "I'm sure that's what my mother always told us. . . ."

I could never forget those two. I'm not sure exactly what they have to do with a book of games, but I'm sure my mother always told us this one was called Someone Beginning with B.

Again this is a variation of a more popular game (Twenty Questions). There are variations of the variation but for now we'll stick with this.

One player—the Lead—thinks of a person or an object. He tells no one. The purpose of the game is for the others by means of earning direct questions to discover who he is. A direct question is of course any question that can be answered by a yes or no. (Are you living? Are you an American? Are you in politics?) The trick here is to earn the right to ask one of these in the following manner.

The Lead starts off by stating that he begins with a certain letter, and the letter he announces will determine all of the questions asked him.

Questions in any one category may be asked three times, no more.

For Example:

Are you a famous composer? (#1)

No, I am not Beethoven.

Are you a famous composer? (#2)

No, I am not Leonard Bernstein.

Are you a famous composer? (#3)

No, I am not Bach.

Enough of that, no more famous composers. It is now the next player's turn and he must move into another category. Let's say, Modern Painters, but again these must all be painters beginning with B.

No, I am not Braque. No, I am not Buffet. No, I am not Bonnard.

A warning: If you ask, "Are you a —?" you had better have one in mind, and one beginning with the letter designated. If you are challenged and you cannot answer, you lose your turn and the game moves on to the next player.

The next player may repeat your question, providing he has an answer in mind, but under no circumstances may the same category be used for more than three questions.

When the Lead is stumped, when he is unable to answer, then the questioner—after stating a correct answer to his own question—has the right to ask directly "Are you living?" or

"Are you fictitious?" or "Are you in the western hemisphere?" —any of these. Remember, your direct question must be formed in such a way that it can be answered by a simple yes or no.

Now that it's written out I'll admit it sounds rugged. It is not. Anyone brought up on Twenty Questions knows that anything on earth can be pinned down. A sister-in-law guessed the remains of Hannibal's elephants once in fifteen direct questions, and my brother discovered I was the current Pope's toe in only twelve.

TWENTY QUESTIONS

Twenty Questions is exactly what the name implies. I say that I am someone or something. I do not have to give you an initial or any hint and through twenty direct questions—questions that I can answer yes or no to—you must discover who I am.

A suggestion: Try being yourself for a round. It's amazing the number of people who'll look right at you and consider Queen Elizabeth, Marlon Brando, almost anyone, before you come to mind.

WHO AM I?

The British have a variation of this which has one great advantage: it offers total participation and can keep a large gathering occupied for hours.

Several things are required. First, someone who has a watch and is willing to be a scorer. Also, you will need some pins and lots of small pieces of paper.

The scorer writes down the names of famous people, characters in history, movie stars, heroines of novels, etc., then the players line up and he pins a name on each back.

The object of the game is to find out who you are. You can ask any other player three direct questions. (Again remember, a direct question is one that can be answered yes or no. Am I a famous statesman? Am I living?) Then in turn you must answer any three he may ask you. Three each, no more, then you move on to ask and answer another player.

When you think you know who you are, you report to the scorer. He will mark down your time, pin another name to your back and send you off again.

It can go on all night, or until the scorer runs out of famous names; the winner being the one who identifies himself most often and in the shortest time.

7: "The Game"

There's no need to write in any detail about "The Game."
Most of us, I'm sure, already know more about it than we
ever cared to know.

Robert Benchley, a confirmed nongame man, was the last
holdout I remember. Everyone in California knew Bench-

ley's feelings; hostesses had been alerted, he would come to dinner only if it was agreed in advance that no one would suggest "The Game." Then one night, as perhaps was inevitable, it happened.

In a house high in the hills above Santa Monica, over after-dinner coffee, suddenly the guests were divided into teams and before the great man could make himself heard, a first round of "The Game" had started.

When his turn came and he was handed a slip of paper— there were at least twenty-five people watching—Benchley blinked several times and adjusted his glasses, but he said nothing. On his slip were the words: Ladislaus Bus-Fekete.

Next Mr. Benchley loosened his tie. Then he moved to the center of the room, got down on all fours and with his right hand indicated a huge circle on the floor. Then he stood, crossed to a hall door and stepped outside.

After a long moment both sides began guessing aloud, searching for a clue.

There was no sound from the hall and the party fell silent again, all eyes staring at the door.

Someone suggested, "A pause . . . a stage wait?"

Time passed.

The hostess grew uneasy. Still there was no sound at the door, no movement, and still no one came up with an answer. Believe me, the wildest guesses were made.

It was almost an hour before the host made a phone call and discovered that Benchley had walked down the hall, out of the house, down the hill to Santa Monica Boulevard. There he had hailed a cab and been driven back to his hotel.

Before starting most games it is suggested that you agree upon rules, but with "The Game" as it is played now—unless you are a revolutionary and want to try getting it back to its original form—signals are more important than rules. After sides have been lined up be sure your team-mates understand the sign language. Some of the more popular signals are:

Pointing to your ear, this means it sounds the same as what's being said.

A thumb and forefinger held close together indicates a short word, an article.

The gesture of slicing a left arm in half with a right hand means that half or a part of a word will be performed.

Wiggling fingers in a come-hither gesture means "You're on the right track, keep on along this line."

Holding both hands above the head and crooking two fingers of each hand suggests a quotation.

Frenetically crossing and recrossing both arms in front of you means "Not at all, you're all wrong, cancel it out and let's begin again."

There's no reason you shouldn't create your own signals. People with limp wrists are often very good at indicating waves rolling on and on, which can mean participles, or "Please add an -ing to what you're saying."

Usually each team selects a captain. A captain's first job is to write down on separate slips of paper the various phrases, quotations, bits of lyrics or what-have-yous that each team thinks up for the opposing team to perform.

When these have been completed the captain of one team will hand to his opposing captain one slip. Without reading it, the second captain will assign this to a member of his own team, who then will study it carefully and on a given signal start acting it out *in pantomime*. No words are allowed by the performer in "The Game." His team-mates, of course, may scream and shout and ask a million questions.

"The Game" is played in rounds, first one team is up, then another. Captains also hold a watch and call "Start" and "Halt" when the opposing team is up. Three minutes is the length of a round and quite adequate for most phrases.

It was Ethel Barrymore who insisted that when young actors auditioned for jobs, thirty seconds was plenty of time. "If they have talent," she said, "you'll know it in thirty seconds. If not, you'll think your watch has stopped."

This can apply to the game as well.

Rounds are timed down to the split second, then are added up. The winning team is the one that has performed all of its assignments in the shortest time.

QUICKIES

This is a variation of the above, which is becoming quite popular in some circles. It does seem to speed things up.

In essence it is the same game played as a relay race with two teams performing simultaneously.

Here someone is selected to function as a judge or a general referee before the game begins. The players then divide themselves into groups with a captain for each team. They retire to opposite sides of the room, exactly as in "The Game." This time, however, the judge sits in the middle with a paper and pencil and makes out a list of names, phrases, and titles. If there are six players on each team, he lists six items, if ten players, ten items, etc. Short phrases are found to be best. Also, proper names should be permissible in *Quickies*.

When the judge's list is complete he calls the two captains to his side and in turn whispers a phrase to each. To the first captain he gives the phrase *at the top of his list*, and to the second the one *at the bottom of the list*. Then on a signal from the judge the captains begin to act out the phrases before their respective teams.

When a member of either team guesses correctly he races to the judge and is given the next phrase which he then must perform for his team. As this one is guessed a third player goes to the judge and so on.

In this way team Number One is working on the phrases as they run from the top to the bottom of the list and team Number Two is working its way up from bottom to top.

Whichever team completes the list first, wins.

Surprisingly both teams you will find are so busy and so

frantically concentrated on their own assignments they never overhear or care about what the opposing team is doing.

Note:

If you have sensed a disapproving, slightly sour tone in this section, you may be right. The basic idea of "The Game" has undergone many changes in the past few years and I am yet to be convinced that all of them are improvements.

The first real change I think was the introduction of signals and the utter dependence of many players on a secret sign language. Along with this there has been a tremendous change in the sort of phrase or quotation one is expected to perform.

The Encyclopaedia Britannica traces the evolution of "The Game" back to French Charades in the eighteenth century, then follows it across to England and the Acted Charades of the early nineteen hundreds. For a description of these one is referred to Thackeray's *Vanity Fair*. Charades, it seems, were in either prose or verse and those of the poet W. Maxwell Pread (1802–1839) are considered by many to be collector's items.

Usually a player recited his Charade, which was a word, divided into syllables with each syllable described as an independent word. (Are you with me?)

Here's a famous example:

My *first* is company.

My *second* shuns company.

My *third* collects company.

And my *whole* amuses company.

Answer:

First syllable—Co (abbreviation of company)

Second syllable—nun (nuns usually shun company)

Third syllable—drum (a drum is one way to collect a company)

Add them all together you get Co-nun-drum.

("My whole amuses company.")

In the late Victorian era (I'm still with the Encyclopaedia), Charades became so popular that "in many circles of the London intelligentsia" elaborate productions were planned weeks in advance with expensive costumes and properties comparable to those used in amateur theatricals. These continued into the twentieth century, although considerably simplified after World War I.

In the United States in the 1930s (now I'm moving out on my own) the Charade turned up in a somewhat different form. It was called Adverbs, or In the Manner of the Word.

ADVERBS

One player leaves the room and the others choose an adverb, preferably one that can be demonstrated in pantomime (clumsily, coyly).

When the first player is called back he asks various individuals to do certain things (carry a book to the piano, ask the hostess to dance) in the manner of the word.

When the correct adverb has been discovered the one who has been guessing names the player who gave it to him, or the one who gave him the most helpful clue to the actual word. This player then goes out and another word is chosen.

VERBAL ADVERBS

Since Adverbs itself is always played in dumb show, you may find that some of your friends—the more vociferous ones —prefer this variation. It has many possibilities.

Instead of asking players to perform specific acts, the one who is guessing asks them to describe something, or discuss a certain topic in the manner of the word.

The other night we'd chosen "angrily" and one of us, a man we'll call F, was asked to talk about politics. Now F is a quiet, affable fellow, usually, but a floodgate seemed to open; the most surprising venom poured out. Another man was told to describe his summer vacation plans and the poor questioner found himself suddenly being attacked. We were all filled with fury, wrath, and deep indignation at his even suggesting such a thing.

Of course it can be pretty bewildering for the one who's trying to get the word. After "angrily" we chose "irrationally," and it appeared that the girl who was out was going to stay out permanently.

She guessed "idiotically," "stupidly," "nonsensically." (In being irrational most of our answers were complete non sequiturs to her. But for those who are in on it, it can be very funny.)

One other thing about Adverbs, if you choose a group of emotionally-charged words it may even take on some of the therapeutic aspects of psychodrama. I know after our round with "angrily" the other night we were all feeling much better, quite fit as a matter of fact. I found I'd probably rid myself of several old resentments I didn't really need.

Adverbs has been around for quite a while and I hope that it stays. The first time I heard about it was in a play of Noel Coward's. The second act of his *Hay Fever* deals with a house party at the home of an aging actress which is thrown into chaos when a group of unsuspecting guests is conned into a round. This may not be the funniest scene Coward ever wrote but you'd have a hard time proving it to the thousands of little-theater groups across the country who have paid their rents—and made Coward quite wealthy—with their annual productions.

Of course, if you've been reared on "The Game," if guessing a lot of meaningless syllables through a series of gymnastic signals is really your dish, all this could seem pretty mild to you. But try one round. It just might be what you're looking for.

At least it will cleanse the palate, and when you return to "The Game" you may find you're more interested in acting out an entire sentence than in frantically pointing to your ear and cutting off your arm.

8: Analogies

I am a lucky man. I arrived in Hollywood during the Hungarian period.

I knew of course that Hungary was a nation of playwrights —most Hungarian boys begin their first comedy in the primary department—and I'd heard that immediately following Munich, trainloads of them had begun turning up on the coast.

I thought I knew what to expect. I'd laughed at all the old gags—"If you have a Hungarian for a friend you don't need an enemy. . . ." I'd read their famous recipe for Chicken Paprika—"First, go out and steal a chicken. . . ." But nothing had prepared me to find so many of them, and all under contract. Between 1940 and 1950, fully half of the paid-up members of the Screen Writers' Guild had unpronounceable names. Another thing I'd not been told was that they are, every last one of them, devout game-players.

The concentrated hard work of writing screenplays is usu-

ally done in the morning hours, say from 10 A.M. to 1 P.M.
This meant that they had the rest of the day and night to
huddle together in the little cubicles of the Writers' Building,
and there they stayed, hour after hour, trying to guess the
identity of obscure historical characters, or figure out exactly
what color Walter Pidgeon was, what music he brought to
mind, what season of the year. . . .

Lazlo S., Bronislaw K., Fedor M., they are scattered now.
Independent producers and television factories have de-
spoiled forever the luxurious leisurely world of L. B. Mayer.
Efficiency experts have caught on that a half-hour western
does not require a year's contract (with an additional six
months for rewrites). The Hungarians have departed, but I
am sure they have found another spot. In some other garden
of random reality they are together, still shedding light, asking twenty questions and making a bloody fortune.

Many of us played Analogies before the Hungarian in-
vasion, but they did lend it a certain flavor, a subtlety all
their own.

It is usually played by one person leaving the room, although I'm in favor of two going out together. It's friendlier
and they can work as a team. The others decide who they'll
be, a famous character or a mutual friend. This doesn't matter, except that it must be someone all of the players know
very well.

The questions the team asks when they are called back
are not direct questions. They must discover by inference
who has been chosen. For example, they will not ask are you
living or dead, but what sound are you? What fabric? What
time of day? Each will discover the analogy that is most
meaningful to him.

Perhaps the best way to catch on is to try a round.

There are two other names for Analogies. One is Essence,
which is very apt, because it is indeed the essence of a per-
sonality that the questions and answers are trying to catch.
The other name is *"If I Were a . . ."* which is aiming at the

same thing. "If I were an object, what object would I be?"
"If I were a period in history, what period . . . ?"

Other categories of Analogies are music, topography,
means of transportation (very telling with some characters),
architecture, weather (I'm afraid a great many people re-
mind me of a summer afternoon, but they are afternoons
when you suspect storm clouds may be gathering in the distance). Others suggest certain animals, certain birds. New
questions are constantly being added to the game.

Now we are moving into those Hungarian subtleties—for
it is not so much what you associate with the person, as what
that person *is* to you. (This is a little difficult to explain, one
of those things you either sense or you don't.) Say we were
being Walter Lippmann and we were asked "What newspaper?" Most New Yorkers, I'm sure, would answer the
Herald Tribune, whereas Mr. Lippmann *in essence* is not the
Trib at all. He is much more an International Edition of
the Emporia *Gazette.*

Somehow the great and the powerful are the most difficult
to pin down. I remember a night when a young fellow was
trying to be Freud. His answers immediately gave us a picture. They fell into such a consistent pattern that we could
have gone on and answered for him. This was clearly an
overwhelming giant. There was a kind of majesty here, a
strength, his music was Wagnerian, he was Michelangelo's
Moses, a burst of light through the darkest clouds. We finally
decided the young man was trying to tell us he was Jehovah
. . . (and so, of course, we lost the round). I've had the same
difficulty being F.D.R.

Another warning, don't ever be yourself. No one will guess
you.

The British have a variation on this, too. They call it Personal Analogies, and indeed it is. They insist that it be done
in writing and only about those present.

Against each name you write down the nearest analogy
you can think of, then you read them all aloud and—I quote

from the book of British rules—"no one need explain why he thinks you are putty-colored or suet-pudding. It is a good way of paying compliments, or settling old scores. . . ."

It is also as good a way of breaking up a party as I can think of offhand.

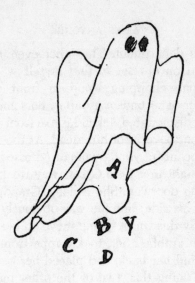

9: *Old Standbys*

The young man looks at his sister and with tears in his eyes asks, "Is it true . . . tell me, is it true you worked as a hustler to send me through college?"

That is a hook. And if you can think of a story that opens with that, or even one that builds up to such a scene, you can be sure of a sale. At least, this is what a famous story editor told me, and this is indeed what I've spent a great deal of my life trying to think up, but hooks, you should know, are not always easy.

"With the right sort of hook," the great man said, "they'll stick with you forever. No matter what drivel or dreary exposition you put in next, the poor suckers haven't a chance. Their attention'll stay riveted, because they have to find the answer to your question."

Television writers, of course, have become the undisputed

masters in this department. The other evening quite inno-
cently I turned on our set to find myself watching a nice
healthy old man chopping wood in front of his house.
Within a matter of seconds a group of horsemen had ridden
into the scene, dismounted, taken his axe from him, and with
no warning whatsoever shot him dead. At the sound of such
commotion a beautiful young woman (dressed rather incon-
gruously I thought in a Kate Greenaway frock and bonnet)
appeared in the doorway. She called, "Grandpa, Grandpa,"
and rushed to his side, but she was obviously too late, and
just as obviously this was a wrong move on her part, because
one of the men grabbed her, took a rope from his belt, tied
her hands behind her back, and placed her across his horse.
While he was doing this, two of the other mischief-makers
had come across an immense can of gasoline. They threw
this at the front porch along with several torches, then as
the group galloped away the camera lingered on a Long Shot
of the old homestead utterly engulfed in flame.

All of this, you understand, happened before the name of
the series appeared on the screen. Of course no one could
turn away. How does a young woman get out of that situation?

If however you are not particularly gifted at hooks, the
next best thing may be to disarm your audience, or so the
same editor told me. By disarm I gather he meant endear
yourself to the public. If, for example, in writing fiction you
see that you're up against a coincidence, don't run from it,
don't hide or try to gloss over it. Come right out and say that
this is one of those hard-to-believe circumstances that occur
so often in real life and so seldom in books.

The theory behind this approach is that by appearing to
be frank and boyishly honest you will so charm the reader
that he'll feel on your side and again he'll be willing to stick
with you through the dreary yet necessary passages that
must follow. Many fine writers, he told me, from de Maupas-
sant to Maugham have employed this ruse.

I can only hope he was right, for that—in case you haven't guessed—is exactly what I'm trying here.

I have no hook. I would not kid you. I can think of no way of seducing you into reading this next set of games as if they were new and original. But they are necessary, they are the standards, the meat and potatoes of a game book.

So if you're an old buff and find that you've been playing most of the games in this chapter ever since Nana held you on her knee, I have only one suggestion: try Speed Reading. That can be a game in itself.

Accredited schools for accelerated reading are popping up at an alarming rate now and each one promises the most amazing results if only we'll enroll.

Apparently my mistake has been that all these years I have been reading *across* the page instead of *down* the page, but now according to the ads, if I will go for one two-hour session once a week, by the end of ten weeks I shall be reading two thousand words a minute. That is two hundred pages an hour. What's more, with a little practice I shall have "excellent retention with magnificent comprehension."

So again, if what follows is old hat to you, try reading down the next few pages and see how your retention is.

Try it. Be my guest.

GHOSTS

Played verbally this is Ghosts, played on paper—or on a blackboard, which is where most of us learned it, I guess—it is Hangman.

The first player gives a letter, the second adds a letter (it may go either before or after the first letter). The third player does the same, etc.

The object of the game is *not* to finish a word. Keep the game going by adding a letter each time your turn comes around.

A completed word ends the game. If you are the one who completed it, or if you find you are unable to add a letter, or if the letter you do add is challenged and you don't have a word in mind (one that appears in the dictionary), then you are declared *one fifth* of a ghost. I know of no other game where ghosts are divided into fifths. (The explanation I've been given is that ghost is a five-letter word, but this does not satisfy me, there must be some other answer.)

Once you become a full ghost you either drop out quietly, or stick around and proceed to annoy the others as outlined on page 22.

For some reason (a very simple reason, I never learned to spell) this has not been a favorite of mine, but I know its appeal. In Africa I watched a group of men become deaf to the sound of enemy planes, utterly oblivious to the maddening ack-ack outside the shelter as they tried to form a word from "o o k k".

And I have seen far better men than I become ghosts because they denied that any word, except possibly "unsouped," could be made out of "n s o u".*

HANGMAN

Someone thinks of a word. He then draws a line of dashes, or blanks, to indicate the number of letters in his word. A rough drawing of a gallows is sketched in beside the blanks.

Player number one suggests a letter. If this is a letter that belongs in the word it is written in above the corresponding

---

* "o o k k" can be developed into bookkeeper, and "n s o u" is on its way to "insouciant."

blank to show its position in the word. If, however, a letter is named which is not in the word, a part of the player's anatomy is added to the noose and the game moves on to player number two, who then tries his luck at guessing another letter.

You must decide, of course, how much detail you'll have in your anatomical sketch. My group settles for six sections (one head, one body, two arms, two legs) but some I know add hands and feet. I've even seen men stay in the game until a hat was added to the corpse. When the figure on the gallows is complete, you are dead. You are also out of the game.

There are several annoying aspects to Hangman and these by all means should be argued out before the game begins. For example, what if the chosen word happens to have three e's (as in serene) and a player suggests an e? Should an e be written in above each blank where it appears in the word, or only once? Try to agree on this in advance.

Another complication has to do with completing another word *within* the given word. Some purists frown on this. For example, let's say the word is ghost. The -ost has already been guessed and a player suggests h (which obviously creates the word host) should this poor player have a part of his anatomy strung up on the gallows, or should he be congratulated and given a chance at another letter? Personally I am against the severity of the innerword school. I find it tough enough to keep adding letters before my whole being swings from a gallows.

GOING ON A TRIP

1st Player: I'm going on a trip and I'm going to take a tooth brush with me. Do you want to come?

2nd Player: I'm going to take some soap along.

1st Player: You can't come with me. I'm also going to take tea bags.

3rd Player:	Can I take tooth paste?
1st Player:	Not with me. Also I shall take two bottles.
3rd Player:	What about thin biscuits?
1st Player:	You can come.
2nd Player:	I'm going mad. Toilet water?
1st Player:	No.
3rd Player:	I shall take some tall boys.
1st Player:	You may come.
2nd Player:	Short boys?
1st Player:	No.

And so it goes. The 2nd Player cannot join the trip until he catches on to the key. In this case, only objects beginning with t— b— are acceptable.

There are as many keys as there are players to think them up. Things beginning with the same letter is a fairly obvious key. The last letter of a word or a certain combination of letters within a word is more difficult.

GRANDMOTHER'S TRUNK (or MY GRANDMOTHER LIKES)

Going on a Trip turns up in all parts of the country under different names. Usually it's played in exactly the same way, but with a variety of lead sentences. "I looked into my grandmother's trunk and there I found a — and a —."

Or simply: "My grandmother likes —."

This can be played with a complicated key *plus* a combination of objects (her likes and dislikes) to indicate what is acceptable and what is not.

"My grandmother likes gin and bitters, but she does not like gin and tonic."

"Does she like books and dislike maps?"

"Yes."

"She also likes ribbons, but she hates laces."

"Yes."

"She likes kettles and hates pans."*

"Yes."

The game ends when all players have discovered the key.

BUREAU DRAWER

Another form of Going on a Trip and Grandmother's Trunk requires no talent for deduction, no search for a hidden key. It's a simple test of memory.

The game proceeds clockwise. The Lead starts with a sentence: "I looked into an old bureau drawer and there I found — (a doll)."

The next player repeats the sentence, word for word, and adds one object: "I looked into an old bureau drawer and there I found a doll and — (a silver spoon)." The third player repeats this, adding his word: "I looked into an old bureau

---

* The old girl apparently goes for things with double letters in them—bitters, books, ribbons, kettles.

drawer and there I found a doll, a silver spoon, and a shrunken head."

Easy enough. For the first ten or fifteen turns. But wait till you are trying to retain in order twenty or thirty unlikely props.

If you miss, or if you make a slip, you are dead and out of the game. Or if you prefer, you are a third of a ghost and are given two more tries.

SUGGESTIONS

This is a slight variation of the Bureau Drawer, and whereas it has overtones of free association, it ends up a taxing memory test.

Someone says a word (usually a noun), the one next to him says another word *suggested* by the first. After three rounds a halt is called and you begin to unwind the chain of suggestions, going backward.

If you go blank or make a slip, you are dead (no waiting to become a full ghost here). You're out and the one next to you carries on, trying to complete the chain in reverse.

THE LOADED TRAY

The following may appear similar to Suggestions and Bureau Drawer, but hold it—very different personalities respond here. A timid, retiring mouse of a man who seemed an utter idiot and dropped dead on the first round of Suggestions may suddenly blossom forth and in fact so take this in his stride he'll wonder what the rest of us find difficult. (Is there something about visual versus auditory memory?)

In another room, unseen by the players, someone places twenty-five objects on a large tray—a book, a pencil, a handkerchief, a key, fairly usual objects. The tray is then brought in to the players and placed where everyone can see it clearly. They are allowed thirty seconds to stare at the tray, no more. Then it is removed and the tray-bearer yells, "Start." Players are given two minutes to write down what they saw on the tray. The one with the most complete list is the winner.

IN PLAIN SIGHT

Another tray containing about fifteen objects this time is placed before the players. But now they are allowed to study it as long as they choose. Then the players leave the room (there's a twist).

The hostess, or any helper she can snare, then plants the objects in various spots around the room, all of them *in plain sight*, but they should be so camouflaged in their new setting that the eye will pass right over them. For example: A wedding ring attached at the end of a lamp cord will never be noticed, a dime resting on any ornate piece of silver, or a fifty-cent piece placed in the center of a glass ashtray can look so like a bit of decoration that very few players will spot it. Color, of course, is a big factor. A pencil standing upright beside a row of books, a handkerchief fitting into the folds of matching drapes, or a fountain pen arranged in a bowl of flowers are often impossible to find.

When all of the objects have been planted, the players are called back, given paper and pencil and a signal to begin.

Here again I am in favor of working in teams—a roomful of competing couples I find much cheerier than a lot of lone wolves sniffing about—but however you decide to play, the object of the game is to discover and write down the exact whereabouts of all fifteen objects.

A little acting ability may come in handy. When you discover your host's key ring fitting neatly into the dials on the TV set, don't scream. Don't jump up and down and point it out to your partner. Saunter casually to another part of the room and in an offhand manner jot it down on your paper.

The first player or team to complete a list wins.

PASSWORD

At the time of writing, Password is enjoying great success as a TV show, which is fortunate; it relieves me of the responsibility of proving that it is possible.

Glancing at the rules written out in a book, you'd swear it would never work. Too much mental telepathy here. And who wants to explain telepathy?

One thing I will say, though. The better you know your opponent, the more familiar you are with his (or her) tables of reference, the easier Password will be for you.

To begin: Think of a word, any word. Write it on a piece of paper and place it in your pocket. Next, by the use of other words, closely related to, or associated with the one in your pocket, you try to guide another player's thinking and make him guess your word. And all of this you must do without actually using the word itself. (Are you with me?)

An example: Say you have written down *lamp*, you might begin by saying *light*.

The other player will answer with the first word that comes to mind; this might be bulb.

He's close, but you've got to pin it down. You try *street*. He answers *people*.

Now he's going off and you must steer him back. You try a wild one, *Aladdin*.

And miraculously he answers *lamp*.

You've done it! You may not know how, but you've done it. And in thirty seconds flat.

There are many ways of playing Password, dividing your group into several small teams, or all sticking together and passing words along in a circle. The most satisfactory method

I find is to have two opposing teams, each with a captain. The captain can collect the slips of paper his team has written out for the opposing team to work on; he also can take care of the stopwatch. In turn, each captain hands over a word to the opposing captain, who will then assign one member of his team to work it into the mind of another member of his own team.

The winning team is the one whose members have guessed all the Passwords they've been handed in the shortest time.

CATEGORIES

Choose a five-letter word. (If you can't think of one to your liking, open the dictionary or Holy Bible and let your finger move along until you come across a word with a comfortable set of letters.)

On a large sheet of paper write the word perpendicularly at the far left-hand side. Next, each player suggests a category—Sports Cars, Patent Medicines, Movie Stars, whatever you like. Write these horizontally across the top of the page.

At a given signal begin filling in under the categories names of persons or things beginning with the letter found in the left-hand column.

After five minutes a halt is called and you start scoring. If ten are playing, no one scores for a word everybody has; if only nine out of ten have it, you each get one point. If eight out of ten, each gets two points, etc., etc.

ADD A LINE (Prose)

On a large sheet of paper the first player writes a few opening sentences for a story. He then folds the paper, hiding everything except the last phrase of what he has written, and passes it along to the next player.

The next player adds two more sentences, folds the paper again, leaving only his last phrase visible and passes it on. A third player does the same, etc.

The story continues around the circle until it returns to the first player, who, without looking at what has gone before, adds one last sentence, bringing the tale he began to a conclusion. The full story is then read aloud.

It sometimes works better and the story has more continuity if you confine yourself to one long sentence:

The first player writes the *name of a woman,* then folds the paper and passes it on.

The second player then writes the word *met* and gives the *name of a man.* He folds the paper and passes it on, as above. (Each player in turn does this, so the next player never sees what has gone before.)

The third player writes *at,* and gives the place of the meeting.

The fourth player writes *she said,* "———————————————————" and fills in the remark.

The fifth player writes *and he said,* "———————————————————" and fills in a reply.

The sixth player begins with the phrase *and so they decided to* ——————————— and he goes on to describe in some detail what they did.

At this point the full sentence is read aloud with each player learning for the first time what was going on before he made his contribution.

ADD A LINE (*Verse*)

A meter and a rhyme scheme must be decided upon before you begin. The first player writes the opening two lines of a poem, folds the paper, leaving only the second line visible and passes it along. Player number two will add his two lines, fold and pass the paper along in the same manner. When all players have made a contribution someone tries reading it aloud.

BOOK REVIEW

This may be for special groups, but when it works, it works quite well. The title of a book is written at the top of a page, it is then folded and handed to a player who adds a subtitle, folds the paper again hiding what he has written and passes it along.

The third player contributes the author's name and a brief opening paragraph from a review of the book.

The fourth player, not seeing anything that has been

written before, gives a choice quotation to illustrate the author's style.

The fifth player does the same, another pithy quotation.

The sixth player gives an opinion of the book, tries to evaluate its chances for commercial success, and signs a reviewer's name.

EDITOR'S DIGEST

This is the reverse of Add a Line. Instead of building onto the preceding player's work, we cut it down.

Each player writes out a story in about one hundred words, no more. This can be an anecdote or an incident he's recently witnessed, anything he likes. When he's finished he hands it to another player whose job is to reduce the story to fifty words. He will write this immediately below what he has received and he may not change the order of any words, or add new ones.

The second player passes his contribution along to a third player, who must boil it down to twenty-five words. The fourth player can use only ten words and the fifth player only five.

At this point, the stories are read aloud going from the five-line version backward to the full hundred-word account.

This may work for a round or two if it's a particularly long weekend and you've tried everything else.

TEAPOT

Coffeepot was ruled out in our house when I was young. And for very obvious reasons. If you remember the game, the group chose a verb—walking, sleeping, brushing your teeth, something simple—then the one who'd been sent out of the room came back and through a series of questions tried to guess the verb. "Do you coffeepot?" "Do boys coffeepot?" "When did you coffeepot last?" "Has Mary ever seen you coffeepot?"

For a while I'm sure our prurient little minds missed the games, but we soon discovered Teapot and this is much better, with infinitely more variety.

As in Coffeepot, one player leaves the room and the group makes the decision, but this time they choose two words, which, although they sound alike when spoken, have quite different meanings; such words as "mail" and "male."

When the questioner is called back he may ask any number of questions of any member of the group. The word "teapot" is always substituted for the word he is seeking.

We used the word "plot" the other night, which was a little rough, because there are three meanings—a secret scheme, an area of ground, and the story of a novel or play.

I was the questioner and I first learned that my hostess owned several "teapots" in the northern section of town; then I was told that when the newspapers deal with "teapots" they are usually mentioned on the movie page or in book reviews.

I was lost, until much later when one of the players began humming an old Rodgers and Hart song ("Thou Swell") which uses the word "plot."

The one who gives the clue that leads to the word is the next to go out and become a questioner.

Some other sound-alikes that we've had luck with are:

> batter
> tart
> sage
> grip, grippe
> pale, pail
> waist, waste
> bear, bare

Warning: Unless your group is talkative and willing to help the questioner along with what may seem extraneous information about their "teapot," the poor man who is out can stay out a lot longer than he cares to. It's no game for "yes" and "no" answers.

DOUBLE WORDS

This is for two or more players. It's very good for those who travel by car and especially night drivers. It will help keep you awake, but I don't think you'll find it so fascinating you will ignore oncoming traffic.

It is based on the incredible number of double words in the language. Someone mentions one of these, for example: "time out."

The next player then takes the *last word* of this pair and makes it the *first word* of another pair, "out strip."

Strip now must be used as the first word of a pair, "strip poker." This can go into "poker face," etc.

You may start with almost any double word and go for a
while before you run into trouble:
  cover charge
  charge account
  account canceled
  canceled check
  check up
  up shot
  shot gun
  gun moll
  Moll Flanders

Moll Flanders
Here you may have an argument. Are proper names per-
mitted? Be lenient for once:
  Flanders Field
  field mouse
  mouse trap
  Trapp family

Whoever says that is definitely out to ruin the game, and
it's up to you whether you'll go on.

If a man misses once he is a third of a ghost, if he misses
twice, two thirds, and the third time he's out. But be sure to
decide about those proper names before you begin.

GOODNIGHT, NOT GOODBYE
One way to end an evening of games is to try to thank
your hostess and carry on a conversation with the parting
guests without using the letter "e."

"It was good playing tonight."

"Happy you was with us. Glad you could stay."

"How about my . . . (not place, not home) my pad for
a round?"

"Good of you to want us to."

Soon you will find you are sounding a little like the heroine

of the movie, *David and Lisa*—poor girl, because of some
frightening experience she could speak only most haltingly
and with a rather strange rhyme scheme—but nothing else
will show you how many "e's" there are in the language.

10: Hit the Leather

KNOW THYSELF

Fortune cookies even in the best Chinese restaurants taste of blotting paper, yet no matter what the choice of desserts may be I order fortune cookies. In the same way, when I see a set of scales in a drugstore or tucked away in the corner of a waiting room—especially one that offers exact weight *plus* a character analysis—I know sooner or later I'm going to step up and drop my penny in.

This weakness, if that's what it is, must be wildly obvious, because in my time I have been pursued by an endless collection of psychics, palm readers, and graphologists. Even in dark cocktail lounges they spot me. The moment I enter they come over with their little flashlights turned on, ready for work.

(Once in Chicago—I hate to admit this—I paid a man a dollar to read my ice cubes. "By studying the fascinating formations in the bottom of a highball glass," a little card said, "Mr. X can ascertain your name, age, and sex." Now considering that most people old enough to be in a bar already know their sex, age, and name, this represents as woeful a waste of a dollar as I can think of.)

I have no idea why my resistance should be so low, but I know I'm not alone in this—gypsies make a very good living. Surely I don't expect any easy cures for my "character defects." What I find in a cookie is never applicable. It seldom makes sense, and the Lord knows the advice I have shoved at me from weighing machines is as depressing as the news that I have gained five pounds. What is the magic word we are always seeking?

If by some unlucky chance you share this weakness, I am sure you will be able to understand my reaction when someone walks up to me—as someone just did—and says, "I have the most *marvelous* new game. It's called Know Thyself. Actually it's much better than a year on the couch . . ."

Time stops right there. No matter what gay chitchat follows it will be meaningless to me until I can get this someone aside and learn the details.

In this case the someone who walked up was Natalie Schafer. Natalie is a rare, ageless girl with a kind of inborn vivacity and a wonderful knack of making anything she suggests doing appear a little more glamorous than it actually is. I am sure if you were with her she could make going to collect unemployment insurance somehow seem the height of chic.

Apparently last summer Natalie played Know Thyself for the first time in Ischia. I have never been in Ischia but I gather it's a magic island where the most beautiful people stretch out on a beach and do nothing but play games. Last summer her little group was joined by a man who turned out to be an Irish nobleman, who had studied psychiatry; furthermore—and I can see no reason not to believe her—he had recently devised a series of questions, which when answered honestly reveal a startling picture of the inner self.

I also gathered that this nobleman was perfectly willing

to play the role of analyst and serve as a general M.C. for the group.

Natalie, of course, made copious notes and they form the basis for the game.

Now before we even list the questions I know you are thinking it's too much to suggest that you find a brilliant psychiatrist in your group. But are you sure?

It sometimes seems to me that we are rapidly becoming a nation of weekend Freuds. Anyone who's had so much as a cousin on the couch seems able to pick up the lingo and feels himself quite qualified to sound off as a headshrinker. Believe me, there is an explosion of amateur analysts in New York this season.

At my barber's only last week I overheard the bootblack asking his boss why he felt so hostile toward him. And at dinner the other night a young man cornered me—a young man who sells Chevrolets during the day—he wanted to know if I'd ever considered the sadistic-masochistic balance in Cinderella. He saw this little story as a case history of sibling rivalries, and good old Prince Charming he'd discovered was a man suffering from a shoe fetish.

When I began to edge away, do you think he minded? Not at all, he smiled with real understanding and said he hoped he hadn't added to my insecurity.

No. If your friends are anything like mine, finding a man to play doctor will not be your problem. Just let them know what the game is. The chances are you may have to use force to weed out the volunteers.

After you've selected your shrinker man let him study the questions, as well as the list of suggestions for interpreting various answers. Then give him some time to practice. He'll probably want to rehearse tilting his head to the side, lifting one eyebrow and in general developing that look of understanding, which will mean, of course, that he is really relating.

The questions should be asked quickly, directly, almost

bluntly, and an effort should be made to get answers in the same way.

Unlike other games (such as Revelations, page 31) there should be no preparation for Know Thyself. The values to be derived here come not from carefully thought-out answers, but from our first spontaneous replies and for that reason the less talk there is about hidden meanings or Freudian implications, the better.

Remember it's the fast response that will give the doctor his insight.

In a large group answers must be written out. In groups of two or three you may try it aloud, but there's always the danger that the overheard answers will influence your honest reactions.

Give only a moment or two between questions. As you will discover a player's readiness to answer—or another's hesitation or quibbling about the meaning of words—may be

very indicative of an inner attitude and prove of great value
to the doctor in his final diagnosis.

Announce it as a psychological test and let 'er rip.

Questions:

1. Describe what your dream garden would be like.

2. What would the house be *in relation* to the garden?

3. What is the key to your house like?

4. What would you do if you found you had lost your key and
wanted to get in?

5. You are standing alone holding an object. Describe the object.

6. At the bottom of your garden there is a property which belongs to someone else. There is a wall around this property
and you discover a gate in the wall and a lock on the gate, but
you have no key for this lock. You very much want to get in.
What would you do?

7. Now you are in. A butler walks up to you and asks what you
would like to drink. What do you answer?

After all questions have been answered, the doctor will
collect them and study each list. Then—and not until then
—he may disclose the fact that his analysis is going to be
based on the following chart:

Interpretation:

1. Your description of your dream garden is your *persona*. It
indicates the front you wish the world to see.

2. Your description of your house and its relationship to the garden describes your real, innermost self and the way you feel
about this self in connection with the rest of the world.

3. The key represents friendships—and let's not go into any
Freudian symbols here. In your description of your house key
there is indeed a key to the simplicity or complexity of your
relationship with most of your friends.

Doctors: See further explanation below.

4. What you do when you have lost your house key discloses

pretty well what you do when something goes wrong in a friendship.

5. The object you choose to describe represents the artistic side of your nature, your imagination.

6. What you do in this situation, when you are up against a wall around your neighbor's property reveals your behavior pattern whenever you are faced with an obstacle.

7. What you say to the butler and the degree of ease with which you say it indicates your social integration. There can be quite a picture here in No. 6 and No. 7 of the way you adjust to unlikely situations.

You may think that there is no game here because all answers will be the same—which, of course, means that you think everyone will answer exactly as you did. But, believe me, the most surprising quirks pop out of the shadows and reveal themselves quite unwittingly, especially if you can capture the first spontaneous answers that come to mind.

Interpreting some of the more bizarre responses may be a challenge, but I am sure if you have been keeping up with the latest paperbacks, or even just stopping in at your local movie house to catch the current spate of psychoanalytic films, you will have no trouble.

Perhaps it would be wise to list a few answers here and indicate some possible interpretations.

For Doctors Only:
Caution—Do not read to players before asking questions. Possibly what follows should never be seen by the patients. Why start arguments?

1. You undoubtedly will find more similarity in the descriptions of gardens than in any of the other answers. The reason for this may be that we are all pretty well agreed on the front we wish to present. We know what is acceptable. If you get a series of banal backyards, rows of roses and tulips, ad-lib as well as you can and quickly move on to No. 2. However, if you bump into a garden with trees bursting in bloom, any refer-

ence to spring or growth, grab this as a symbol of health. (People love to hear that even their masks are in good shape.) Also you may find an age differential working here. The young are often much more ambitious; they dream of more formal (hence more difficult and more expensive) gardens. As we get on we envision gardens we know we can cope with; weeds and the inevitable mistakes of nature do not bother the aged. Our fronts to the world need not be so meticulously manicured.

2. The inference in the relationship of one's home (one's self) to the garden is fairly easy to interpret. Most people imply that the house is secure and "looks out on the garden." But occasionally you will run across a character who insists his house is on a hill *above* the garden, or completely *removed* or *shut off* from it. Nod knowingly here, indicate you find this highly significant, and I promise you you'll establish instant rapport. The rest of the evening will be a breeze.

3. Most people have ordinary keys, "like everyone else's," they are solid, serviceable, standard sets of keys and perfectly dependable. But you may find someone who goes into the most incredible detail, with a minute description of its shape, how long he's owned it, etc., etc. I know one man who had his house keys copied by Cartier; he now has a set of solid gold duplicates (one who places great value on friendship, I presume). But how you diagnose a girl who says "I have no keys, I never had any, doors should not be locked" I've no idea. You're on your own with that one.

4. How one reacts when something is amiss in a friendship (or when a house key is lost) is immediately revealed here. The fretters, the complicated worriers stand right out, so do the direct-action boys. Poor Mona S. knew that she'd be furious, but she had no idea what she would do. She might phone Steven, or she might be able to stay with the Hendersons, but she'd never disturb them if it were late. . . . On the other hand, George Oppenheimer gave the fastest, most direct answer I have ever heard: "I'd call the janitor. Of course." I'm sure he would, and I'm sure there are few interpersonal relationships George wouldn't handle in quite the same way.

5. In the description of the object one is holding you may find you've tapped analytic gold, or you may be left standing with egg on your face and absolutely nothing to say. Objects cover the full gamut from the unprintable to the Hope diamond. If you're fortunate, something will be mentioned which ties in with a player's career—"my violin," "a paintbrush," or "the script of a brand-new play." These are indeed symbols of artistic aspirations. One man mentioned wood-carving tools, and I was lucky, it turned out he'd secretly dreamed of someday becoming a cabinetmaker, but with other answers you may have to dig pretty deep to find their significance. "A vase with one rose in it," for example, leaves me pretty baffled, but when a young writer said he imagined himself "holding a baby who was reaching up with both hands" I found I was able to improvise for quite a while. Evolution, ambition, the yearnings of mankind, all were touched upon. And all to his utter delight.

6. You can handle your diagnosis here along the same lines as in No. 4. The way one surmounts the obstacle of his neighbor's wall, or the way he surrenders before it, is a very basic blueprint of an inner attitude and can be read as clearly as an X-ray plate. The complications which some people create will amaze you. They'll go for a ladder, but where will they find one? They'll climb trees and wonder if it will be safe to jump such a distance. . . . But again there are the Oppenheimers. "What would you do?" "I'd climb the wall. Of course."

7. What one says when the butler approaches and asks what you'll have to drink is always my favorite answer and I'm always being surprised. The most unlikely people know exactly what they want and have no compunction about asking for it. Others whom I'd have said would be at ease anywhere, the perfectly adjusted ones, will hem and haw and almost apologize to the butler. The other night I was very touched when a friend of mine admitted he wouldn't ask for anything. "You see, I wouldn't feel I should be there really. I'd be intruding and I wouldn't want to trouble the butler." This was the answer of a man I thought I knew, a man I had watched in all sorts of situations and had seen conducting himself with poise

and—or so I thought—the greatest self-assurance, yet this was his initial response.

Maybe if you look at the answers others give and get a chance to study them, you'll want to change the title. Maybe it should be Know Thy Neighbor.

11: Mad, Mad Words

ANAGRAMS

I had always thought that anagrams went out with caraway biscuits, tea at the Vicar's, and smelling salts, but I couldn't have been more wrong.

On a flight from Los Angeles recently I found myself sitting beside a member of the jet set. He introduced himself as an international banker, and then after I'd watched him polish off two double-crostics—he did these *in ink* by the way, which I must say struck me as the height of ostentation—I noticed him take a pad from his pocket and begin unraveling a complicated series of scrambled words. Still later as we ambled thirty thousand feet above Chicago he challenged me to a round of Word Hikes.

Now in case you're thinking I had come across an eccentric, or some sort of throwback, believe me, you are as out of touch as I was. This man was a talker, and as he described his world I learned that word games are "very large" on the Continent this season, as well as in various sections of the U. S. A.

In fact he told me that whenever business took him to Nevada he was able to pick up a considerable piece of change playing anagrams. That took care of tea with the Vicar.

My new friend furthermore had theories about this trend. One was that in word games modern man has found a sense of orderliness that is missing in the rest of his life. Every puzzle poses a question which has a definite and provable answer. (And just how many of these do we run into now?)

Frankly I am an amateur, a Johnny-come-lately to the whole family of word problems, but I understand the attraction. It's not unlike what I feel for bad novels; especially when I'm tired there's a sense of security in knowing that in the world of the novel at least it is still possible for things to work out.

I had one other misapprehension about anagrams. I not only believed they'd died out with Grandmama, I thought they'd started as a Victorian parlor game. Not at all. They date back to ancient times.

This trick of transposing the letters of a word (or words) so they will produce other words was more than a mere pastime to the Greeks and Hebrews. They believed there was a mystic connection between things and their names and that by concentrating on them and turning their letters inside out important secrets of nature might be revealed.

For some reason this struck the ancient Romans as nonsense. We have inherited no anagrams from them, which does seem strange since Latin—being utterly free of k's, j's, and z's, those letters that are the bane of every game-player's life—remains the perfect language for puzzles. Yet it's true, you will find all great Latin anagrams are the creation of modern scholars.

By the middle ages, however, they were back in good favor. So much so that certain astronomers, fearing their discoveries might be filched, are known to have hidden their findings in anagrammatic codes. They swept Europe, and by the seventeenth century in France they'd achieved such popularity that Louis XIII had to create a special office, "anagrammatist to the King" and all sorts of writers were deriving pseudonyms from rearrangements of their family names. (The most famous of these of course is Voltaire, which still strikes me as stretching a bit. His name was Arouet, and by adding two letters l.j.—for *le jeune* or the younger—he came up with Uoltajre, which is no name at all. But by assuming that u equals v and j equals i he arrived at Voltaire.)

In England in the seventeen hundreds anagrams were driving men mad—literally. There is one sad story of a young lover who retired from the world to see if he could form an anagram out of his mistress' name, then when he finally hit upon one and returned to society he learned that her name was not spelled Chumley as he had supposed, but Cholmondeley, he went off his rocker and spent the rest of his days in Bedlam.

If you find this excessive, or if you agree with the Romans that it's so much nonsense, still you must admit an anagram is not easy. Dryden dismissed them as "the torturing of one poor word ten thousand times," and even this is not exaggerating. A mathematical friend of mine has figured out that any word of twelve letters (or any two words of six letters) can yield more than 729,000,000 transpositions.

Considering that figure—no matter how childish or Victorian I may have thought them—I now look upon the following examples with a kind of awe.

As in all word games you will find there are the rigid purists, who allow no additions, no omissions or changes, and there are also more lenient players who don't mind adding an occasional y or e, if it will bring about a happy solution.

For the purists among you I know of no better example than the three little words someone discovered in the letters of "revolution" and "radical reform":

revolution—love to ruin
radical reform—rare, mad frolic

Some other examples which seem particularly meaningful to me because the anagram in each case is so closely related to the original word are:

Astronomer—moon starer
Christianity—I cry that I sin
Crinoline—inner coil
Parishioners—I hire parsons
Payment Received—every cent paid me
Presbyterian—best in prayer

Also I am sure there must be a special thrill in getting a meaningful phrase from proper names such as:

Marie Antoinette—tear it, men, I atone

Florence Nightingale—flit on, cheering angel

Victoria, England's Queen—governs a nice quiet land

Someone—and I wish I knew who—found that hidden in the letters of Pilate's famous question there was indeed an answer to that very question:

Quid est veritas? (What is truth?)

Est vir qui ad est. (It is the man before you.)

There is one distressing thing in writing about great anagrams—there is no possible way to acknowledge their originators. As they are passed on from generation to generation—in some cases from century to century—no one seems to recall who created them. Such masterpieces should not float through history authorless.

Think of the pride one of our ancestors must have had when he rearranged the letters in

"Washington crossing the Delaware"

and found that he'd come up with

"He saw his ragged Continentals row."

That man's name should be remembered.

PALINDROMES

A palindrome is a word or sentence which may be read letter by letter backward as well as forward.

They have been called a species of anagrams, but believe me, unless you're content to play around with a few individual words—civic, noon, tenet—they are infinitely more difficult. I'll even go so far as to say that if in one lifetime you are able to create one simple sentence that is a perfect palindrome, yours is a life well spent.

Unfortunately, as with anagrams, there is no way to give

PALINDROMES

credit to the original authors. These are the anonymous gifts of history.

The following is a perfect example; it is also my favorite because I like to imagine that it was the first line of dialogue spoken on earth:

Madam I'm Adam.

The next one has been attributed to Napoleon himself, but whoever thought it up did a masterful job:

Able was I ere I saw Elba.

Another, possibly inspired by the above is:

Snug & raw was I ere I saw war & guns.

Those two &'s pull it down a notch from perfection but there's nothing wrong with this simple sentence:

Name no one man.

Or with the slightly more cumbersome:

Lewd did I live, evil I did dwel.

(Unless of course you're going to be a rigid purist about I's.)

Again, as with anagrams, Latin seems to be the most flexible language. The Oxford English Dictionary tells us this one first appeared over the porch of a free school in 1638:

Subi dura a rudibus.

The next one has been around a long time, but it might serve as a motto for a lawyer today:

Si nummi immunis. (If you pay, you'll go free.)

But all anagrams, all palindromes, all word scrambles pale beside the following, which is unique in many ways. It can be read backward and forward as well as upward and downward:

s a t o r
a r e p o
t e n e t
o p e r a
r o t a s

If this floors you (as it should) and you're deciding to bow out now and leave the whole subject with the Latin scholars, let me tell you palindromes are still turning up. Modern ones may be simpler than *sator, arepo,* etc., but many of them are quite perfect in their own way.

Last winter a Mr. Robert F. Kolkenbeck of Pelham, New York, sent in two to the Sunday *Times.* The first, he said, was a tribute to the man who completed the Panama Canal, George Washington Goethals:

A man, a plan, a canal . . . Panama

The other was inspired by Mr. Kolkenbeck's father, who mentioned one evening that he had seen a travel ad for Trinidad on the Lexington Avenue subway:

Dad in I.R.T. sees Trinidad

If the above still seems too rarefied—as it certainly does for me—you might like to come down to earth and test your word skill on a practice course of Hidden Anagrams (sometimes called Scrambled Words) or Word Hikes. It is impossible to imagine a way to play Palindromes as a competitive game, simple anagrams may be worked out by teams in the same way that two people can solve a crossword puzzle or a double-crostic, but the following are proper games, it is possible for someone to win a round.

These can be lots of fun in small groups, and for some reason they are especially well suited to travelers.

AIRBORNE SCRABBLE (or HIDDEN ANAGRAMS)

My friend on the plane first handed me a list of words. Each of these, he said, could be transposed into another word by adding one letter. I remember two from his list:

cantos—with an i

pouches—with a y*

Next he explained a Las Vegas version of this. You exchange with your opponents lists of "scrambled words." These words may or may not make sense, that is up to you.

The purpose of the game is to restore the original word, and the player who does this in the shortest time is the winner.

With Airborne Scrabble, he pointed out, it is wise to give hints (and he was quite right). For example, he suggested using words that belong in the same category and mentioning what the category is. All of the words on my list, he told me, contained the names of flowers:

love it

I trust u man

chummy anthers

("Love it" is fairly obvious, it transposes into violet. "I trust u man" goes into nasturtium, and "chummy anthers" can become chrysanthemum.)

---

* Cantos with an "i" can be transposed into canoist, and pouches with a "y" can become chop-suey.

WORD HIKES

Down the right- and left-hand sides of a sheet of paper make lists of words of four, five, or six letters. If possible arrange the words that are opposite one another into pairs that have some obvious connection, such as:

work   play
love   hate

The purpose of the game is to change all of the words in column one into their opposite word in column two.

Each time a letter is altered you have taken a step, and every step must produce an English word, a word you can find in the dictionary.

After a set time, papers are compared and the player who has completed his hike (his list) with the fewest steps is the winner.

You will want to make up your own lists, and of course you may use as many letters in each pair as you choose. Here are a few simple ones to practice on:

pups   dogs
puss   cats
fresh   stale
warm   cold*

Warning: In all word games always use pencil. You'll find even with a pencil at some point there are so many erasures you won't be able to go on. But who knows, at this point perhaps you should give up words and go to bed. After all, the Romans had no time for them.

* *work to play* takes five steps: work, pork, park, pare, pale, play . . .
love to hate takes three steps: love, hove, have, hate . . .
pups to dogs, four steps: pups, puns, guns, song, dogs . . .
puss to cats, three steps: puss, pass, pats, cats . . .
fresh to stale, five steps: fresh, shelf, shell, spell, pelts, stale . . .
warm to cold, four steps: warm, ward, card, cord, cold.

12: A Mixed Bag

Let the word get out that you are preparing a book of games and suddenly you are the most popular kid on the block. Friends you haven't heard from in years will phone to tell you you *must* include their game. There's never a question of whether you care for the game or not, they *know*.

Did you ever notice what particular things people advise you about? (I'm not sure that we couldn't make a game out of such a list.) Very few I find go at your clothing, or the appearance of your family. Uncle Ted may look like Dr. Jekyll after a night on the town, but most people will come to dinner, meet old Uncle Ted and never mention his appearance. Also, hardly anyone criticizes food. You can serve peanut butter canapés, followed by the most unedible meal —they'll down it with nary a comment. The same thing goes for the drinks you mix, your pets, your furniture, but not for pictures. Here every man is an authority and seems to feel you've been sitting around waiting for his opinion.

On the coast ten years ago—at a time when there was some money in the bank and when also the asking price for pictures was half what it is today—I was able to collect a group of Picasso lithographs. Since I am fond of these and consider them, quite seriously, among the great graphics of our time, they hang on the wall wherever I am. But in these years I've had to develop the trick of not hearing what people say. And by people I mean everyone, from close friends to delivery boys. "Oh, I didn't know you were an artist" is a not infrequent opener, or "Tell me, how long have you been drawing, Bob?"

There was a certain comfort in the news that not only collectors but Picasso himself runs up against this sort of thing. Apparently one afternoon the local postman wandered into the studio at Vallauris and stood for a long moment before a group of mammoth canvases, then he smiled sweetly. "Ah," he said, "I see the little fellow paints, too. How old is your boy, monsieur?"

This may or may not be true, but in New York certainly my friends not only know what they like, they know all about art. And all about games, it would seem.

At first, since most of the games in this chapter were suggested by others, I thought of calling it "But Not for Me," but that seems to imply that I have tried them and in some way have found them wanting, which is not accurate. (Do you also wonder, when you see a giant book of games, or an eight-hundred-page cookbook, if the author has tested all the ingredients? I wonder, but I no longer ask out loud. Once when I was quite young I had the privilege of visiting Alexander Woollcott, and I still can remember how impressed I was at the endless rows of books in his library. I made the mistake then of asking if he had read them all, and Woollcott gave the only possible answer. "Some," he said, "I have read twice.")

So far I can say honestly that I have played every game listed here more than twice. But what follows now is indeed a mixed bag.

These have one common denominator—they were all someone else's idea. Playing them I cannot think will win the cold war, they will not solve any of our pressing national problems, nor I'm afraid will they alter your attitude toward your fellow players. If you're a misanthrope when you start on these, a misanthrope you will remain.

Robert Wallsten who suggested the first one is a man with a rare combination of talents, he writes well and he reads magnificently, especially classic verse. Recently Bob gave a reading of Macbeth before the student body of Avon Old

Farms in Connecticut. At the end of the evening a lad of ten walked up to him, shook his hand firmly, and said he wanted to thank him. "I love to hear tragedy," the boy went on, "because you see, sir, there is so much comedy in real life."

I'm afraid nothing in this chapter would effect such an outlook.

YOU'VE GOT A FACE

A player begins by turning to the one on his left and saying, "You've got a face," to which the second player replies, "What sort of face?" and player number one answers (for example), "A fabulous face."

Player number two turns to the one on his left and says, "You've got a face." And so the game goes around the room, with each player answering the question, "What sort of face?" with an adjective beginning with f, or with the same letter the first player used. Any letter will serve for a round, but you must stay with that letter, and you must answer when your turn comes.

The point is to establish a rhythm, and as fast a rhythm as possible.

At first this may sound like a childish roundelay, but have patience. You will soon find that as the conscious mind starts to run out of adjectives beginning with a certain letter the subconscious is there ready and waiting to speak up with the most surprising supply.

As the rhythm picks up and each player knows he must answer I have seen husbands look at first fascinated, then fearful, then furious at what their wives may come up with next.

A *Variation:* After you've played several rounds with the same letter, try going down the alphabet. The first player will use an adjective beginning with *a* (an attractive face), the second player will describe a *b* face (a bucolic face), the third a *c* face and so on around the room, using adjectives beginning with the consecutive letters of the alphabet.

MURDER
Actually this can be played in a simple two-room apart- ment, but to hear most people describe their experiences

with Murder, you'd think it required an ancestral mansion the size of Manderley or Tara.

Any room or any series of rooms that can be blacked out will serve quite well.

First one player is selected to be a detective (in some groups he's called the D.A.) and the success of the game, you'll find, depends on your astuteness in casting this role. You will want someone with imagination, capable of asking a series of probing questions as well as the sagacity to interpret the answers, distinguish fact from fiction and phony alibis from simple truths. In short you want Nero Wolfe.

After the detective has been chosen, folded slips of paper, one for each of the other players, are placed in a hat. All of these are blank except one, which is marked with a large X. Next the hat is passed around the room and each player draws a slip, examines it, and then hides it somewhere on his person. Great care should be taken not to let anyone see your slip, or to disclose in any way who has drawn the X.

At this point, several minutes may be allowed to pass—time to refill drinks or take another helping of dessert—before the detective crosses to the switch, blacks out the playing area, and moves on to another part of the house to wait until he is called.

In the darkness players may move about or stay put; they may do whatever they choose. But now the one who has drawn the X will commit his crime. He can do this immediately, or he can wait awhile to get his bearings and create his alibis, but the crime itself is always performed in the same way. The man with the X (the murderer) approaches another player and places his hands around his throat. He may hold his victim for a few seconds, no more, then he must release him.

As soon as the other player (the victim) feels the hands at his throat he will scream and fall to the floor, no matter where he happens to be at the moment.

There is usually a certain commotion after a murder, but upon hearing the scream the detective re-enters, turns up the lights, and begins his questioning.

Exactly when he decides to come back is up to the detective—some prefer to wait for things to settle down, others like to spring immediately into action. Of course, if he seems to be taking too long any player should feel free to call him. (Would the murderer call for a detective? Very possibly he might.)

From here on the group places itself completely in the detective's hands and he has unlimited authority to question anyone in whatever manner he chooses.

The game ends when the detective, having collected what he considers sufficient evidence, makes a formal accusation. The accused then must produce his hidden slip and we learn just how astute the law has been.

One thing must be borne in mind during the questioning, if any progress is to be made. With the exception of the murderer himself, everyone in the group wants to be a cooperative witness, wants to see the true criminal brought to justice and therefore will answer any and all questions as honestly as he can. Only the murderer will lie.

A Suggestion: If you draw the X slip, it is a very good idea to stay close by another player, preferably—if you're a man —an attractive female. When the lights go out and the group starts milling about take the lady's hand in yours, in your left hand, and never so long as the lights are out let go of it. In this way your right hand can remain free and that is all you'll need.

When a likely victim moves close enough, place your free right hand on his throat. He'll scream and drop to the floor, but you have a solid witness on your side, a girl who will swear that you are innocent. She'll be convinced of this because she was holding hands with you the entire time.

MY SHIP

Deep inside me something knows that right now there are two hundred men at their typewriters. In offices and libraries across the country they are hard at work eighteen hours a day, seven days a week, and every one of them is writing a game book. These brilliant works will appear in bookshops at the very same time as this little volume.

There is no point in trying to laugh it away; my competitor syndrome has been around for years.

When I was young and the world seemed filled with even more such characters, I stumbled across a very comfortable way of handling them. I chartered an ocean liner and had it sail out of New York Harbor every year on the first day of June.

This was a fine seaworthy vessel. There was only one thing about it, it never docked anywhere, it just sailed on and on. No one aboard came to any harm, he simply never returned.

I, of course, was the passenger agent and through the long winter months I made up my lists. Usually these were men who'd got the jobs I felt I should have had, well-known bores around town and people who owed me money. In time friends caught on and would give me their lists, but I was Mr. Fullcharge and all final decisions were mine.

I bring this up now because I just found out that the British have a game, Sleighs, that is not unlike My Ship. To me there are several important differences, but apparently they have been playing this in one form or another for generations.

SLEIGHS

This can be played only in groups where the players have a great many of the same friends.

First each one makes a list of ten friends, the ten closest, dearest friends you have in common. Next you imagine you are crossing Siberia in a blinding snowstorm. You and your friends are in a sleigh and the sleigh is being followed by a pack of starving wolves. Now your problem is this: the weight of your gay group is too much for the troika and you find you must throw someone off. Whom do you throw first? Whom next?

You make up your mind and number the names on your list in the order you would sacrifice them.

A rule of the game is that you may not toss yourself to the wolves.

When everyone has completed this ghoulish job the numbers you have placed against the names are added up. The man with the lowest number beside his name is declared the most unpopular of your friends.

End of game.

Among that group of two hundred competitors mentioned above I am sure that someone is doing a chapter on national characteristics as revealed in parlor games. I would not try to move onto his turf, but I am curious about the next one, also from England.

SACRIFICES

A piece of paper on which is written the names of all those present is passed around the room.

This time you are to imagine an ancient god of vengeance and you are told that he can be pacified only by the human sacrifice of someone who is present.

Again you go down the list and make a mark opposite the one you'd offer up first. When the list has been to everyone the player who has the greatest number of marks against his name leaves the room and the list starts around again.

Those still alive choose their next victim and in turn he is sent away.

When it gets down to the last two they discuss the matter from all points of view, which one has contributed most, their future potentials, etc., etc. Then they call the others back and announce their decision. The one who survives I gather is the winner.

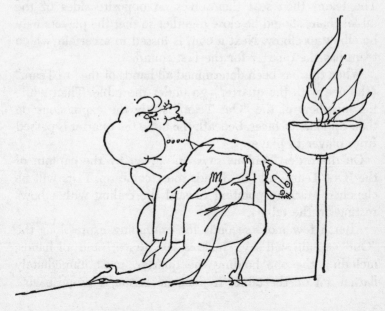

~arlier I said that a certain game (Personal Analogies) was as good a way as I knew to break up an evening. I was wrong. One quick round of Sacrifices would split any group on earth.

If played seriously husbands would turn on wives, brothers on sisters, the most doting mother would be revealed a howling Lady Macbeth.

I sometimes wonder about the British.

JENKINS UP

Divide your group, or your family, into teams. This is a fine game for large family gatherings because all ages, all dispositions can get a workout here.

Only two things are needed, a dining room table (or its equivalent) and a twenty-five cent piece.

First a captain is chosen for each team—and this should be done with some care since in Jenkins Up many orders are given, but only the orders of the captains are to be obeyed. The teams then seat themselves on opposite sides of the table; chairs should be close together so that the players may be elbow to elbow. Next a coin is tossed to ascertain which team has the quarter for the first round.

When this has been determined all hands of the "In Team" (the one with the quarter) go under the table. Then while the members of the "Out Team" study the expressions on their opponents' faces, beneath the table the quarter is passed from player to player.

On the order "Jenkins says up" given by the captain of the "Out Team" all "In" hands must come up. Fists will be clenched (usually pointing toward the ceiling with elbows resting on the table).

After a few more seconds for examining expressions the "Out" captain will say, "Jenkins says *down*," and all hands, including the one holding the quarter, must immediately flatten out on the table. If done in unison, I promise you, there will be such a resounding smack that it will be impossible to tell exactly where you heard the quarter hit the table.

At this point some "Out" player will be sure that he's spotted the quarter, but a wise captain will wait until he has given a few more orders.

Again orders are to be obeyed *only if they come from the captain*. If another "Out" player gives a direction and an "In" follows this direction, that "In" is immediately dropped from the game.

Captains, of course, will make up their own orders, but two of the best ones are:

"Jenkins says creepums, crawlums" meaning with palms flat on the table all fingers are to be lifted and wiggled in a crablike motion.

"Jenkins says dance 'em, prance 'em." This is not easy. The quarter first must be maneuvered into the center of the palm and held securely there, next the hand is lifted into a position where only fingertips rest on the table and the fingers themselves are at right angles to the palm. It can be done, you can even dance and prance your hand around in this position, but practice.

Between each order captains will consult with teammates. If several are convinced they know which player has the quarter the captain will name that player. If he is right, the quarter is forfeited. If wrong, the "In" hands go under the table again and you're off on another round.

Orders always must be preceded by "Jenkins says . . ." Captains may try to trick their opponents by snapping "Up!" "Down!" "Creepums, crawlums" but if a player obeys an order that is not what Jenkins says, he's dropped from the game.

Scores can be kept by adding up the number of wins or by counting the hands left on the table at the conclusion of each round.

A word of advice, remove all rings, watches, and bracelets before you begin. Also if your family is anything like mine, set a time limit: Small children must be in bed by midnight. And stick to it.

13: Stunt Men and Mystics

There are two attitudes one may adopt toward party mind readers. You may, of course, try to suffer them gladly, or—and this has had to be my motto for years—if you can't lick them, join them.

Certainly there is no reason now to think you can avoid them. They are everywhere and their number is increasing. Sooner or later—unless we move in very different circles—one will turn up and announce that he is clairvoyant, then to prove his point, he'll offer to leave the room and let you select an object, a person, or a word. When he comes back, after a few questions have been put to him, he'll tell you exactly what you've chosen. Like all con men, the party mystic works with a confederate; the "medium" uses a "control" to ask him questions, and it is in these questions—or in the order in which they are asked—that the secret lies.

Of course, all signals must be studied and agreed upon before the performance.

What follows are various secret codes that I have been collecting over the years for the sole purpose of meeting these jokers on their own ground.

FOUR-LEGGED OBJECTS

Let's say the group chooses Harry's ring. The medium returns and his confederate starts asking, "Is it my hat?" (No) "Is it this book?" (No) "Is it Helen's poodle?" (No) "Is it Harry's ring?" (Yes)

He can't miss, because he and the questioner have decided

in advance that it will be the first object mentioned after something with four legs (in this case, Helen's poodle).

Once more: Helen's purse has been selected. "Is it my tie?" (No) "Is it this chair?" (No) "Is it Helen's purse?" (Of course!)

That is a pretty simple system, but it will do for openers. Many others are developments of this basic code. The trick is to be able to alter the code whenever you notice that someone is about to catch on.

Smaller Than a Dime is a variation of Four-legged Objects that I've had great success with. It follows the same pattern. The correct answer is whatever comes immediately after the mention of an object that is smaller than a dime.

For example, the control asks, "Is it this lamp?" (No) "Is it the dining room table?" (No) "Is it my coat?" (No) "Is it this button on my shirt?" (No) "Is it the martini shaker?" (It is)

This was the first thing mentioned after a shirt button, which is almost always smaller than a dime.

The Word Codes used for guessing names and places may be as simple, or as complicated, as your mind can cope with. Here are some simple ones, you complicate them.

The group chooses a state, Ohio. When the medium returns, the control asks:

Is it Maryland?
No.
Maine?
No.
Pennsylvania?
No.
North Carolina?
No.
Ohio?
Absolutely!

This is the first state mentioned after a double-word state.

I have seen this done by the control at first mentioning only states that lie above the Mason-Dixon line, then when he asks about one south of the line, the medium knows this is *the key*, the next state mentioned after this will be the chosen state.

Some confederates use the first letters of states and run up and down the alphabet—Arizona, California, Pennsylvania, South Dakota—then, when they reverse themselves and throw in Connecticut, that is the key.

The number of signals that may be given by *physical movements*, or the posture a control assumes when the game begins, is infinite. No book could list them all.

These are most often used for guessing which object or which player the group has selected; but if a medium and a control have time to rehearse together, there is no reason a system can't be worked out to identify almost anything, certainly any card in the pack.

For example:

The group separates the cards (face up) on a table, selects one and then calls the medium back.

He will first glance at his confederate. If he sees him scratching the left side of his chest he will know the card is a heart; if his hand is in his pocket, it's a diamond; if he immediately stands up, it is a club; if he sits, it's a spade.

The suit is now set. The medium crosses to the table and studies the cards. The next time he glances at his confederate, he'll be given the exact card. If one hand is resting on a piece of furniture, it's a deuce. If one arm hangs loosely at his side, it's a three; if both hands are hanging, it's four, and so on and so on. It's better to think up your own signals.

This is a lot of work, but sometimes it's worth it.

VIBRATIONS

One simplification of the above baffled me for years. A girl I know is telepathic (she says) and quite often she will ask her friends to choose a number, any number from one to fifteen, then she leaves the room while they do this.

When she comes back she tells us to concentrate on the number. Next she begins to move about placing her fingers on each of our temples. She usually receives her thought wave quickly and she is invariably right.

One night, however, we found ourselves with a group of total strangers, and she was forced to ask me to stand in for her regular confederate. (This is the only way I learned her trick.)

It could not be simpler. We had chosen the number 4, and when she placed her fingers on my temples, I clenched my teeth four times.

She said nothing at that moment. She moved on to the next man (clever girl), looked deep into his eyes and announced very quietly that we were thinking of the number 4.

Try it yourself, place your fingers on your own temples, clench your teeth and feel the movement each time you do.

PASS THE SCISSORS

Still another hidden code that is based on the simplest of physical movements kept me guessing for hours.

This is not one for a medium and a control. It works a lot better if several of you know what you're doing. The others have some chance then of catching on.

Gather the players in a circle. Take a pair of scissors and hand them to the player on your left. As you do this, say to him, "I received these scissors uncrossed, I pass them to you crossed."

He is now to hand them to the player next to him with a correct description of how he received them and how he is passing them on, "crossed" or "uncrossed."

The trick turns out to have nothing to do with the condition of the scissors—though I can promise you they will be examined, they will be opened, closed, turned upside down, pointed in, pointed out, passed along with the left hand, the right hand.

It is impossible not to think that the words "crossed" and "uncrossed" refer to the scissors.

In actuality, you are describing the position of your feet at the time you receive the scissors and at the time you pass them on.

To drive the more earnest players mad, one of you—one who is in on the secret—can make a great to-do about opening and closing the scissors before passing them on. He also may cross his feet *after* he receives them and so be able to say quite honestly, "I received these scissors uncrossed. I pass them to you crossed."

WHO OWNS THIS? and *PHOTOGRAPHY* use exactly the same signal, but some mystics like to try a round of each.

When the medium is out of the room, the control is given an object that belongs to one of the players—preferably something that is unfamiliar to most of those present. The control holds this in his hand and when the medium is called back, he asks, "Who owns this?"

The medium will study the object and then begin to concentrate on the various players. He will always come up with the right answer—always, if he remembers the signal —because his control will take the exact same position as the owner of the object.

In *PHOTOGRAPHY* the medium calls himself a photographer and while he is out of the room, the group decides which one of them is to be photographed. The medium's confederate can be helpful here in getting everyone into photographic poses before the photographer is called in.

When the medium returns he will study the group, then immediately point to the one whose picture he'll take.

The tip-off is that the assistant has assumed the same pose as the player the group decided upon.

For some reason this was a favorite game of my grandfather's, and as the head of the house there was never any arguing about it, he was always the photographer.

After Sunday night suppers he'd step out into the hall and the family—oh, there were a great many of us—would have to drape ourselves about the dining room in naturalistic poses.

As we grew up we each in turn would be tapped as his assistant. But he never seemed to realize that we had played the game before, or that on our own we might have guessed the secret.

I shall never forget one night when he was called back— we were all grown by then and something evil in us had decided to put an end to the game.

The old man stood dumbfounded, looking at his family. There was no possible way for him to be given a signal. We, every one of us, were lined up in exactly the same pose.

It ended the game, but I think it may have had something to do with ending him, too. He never suggested a mind-reading act again.

LONDON FOUR, VENICE TWO

There is one other secret code, which may sound too complex at first, but stick with it, it's very simple and through it the most unlikely bits of information may be passed along.

The entire key is in the title. Remember this and what it means and you're in business.

Let's say that the word you're trying to transmit is *love*. You might begin by saying that you're going on a trip and that you plan to be in London. (This is a place-name and the first letters in place-names indicate the consonants of your word—in this case, the letter "l".)

Next you say you will be there four days. (Here is the first number you have mentioned and in this game a number refers to a vowel. The number 4 indicates the fourth vowel: a, e, i, *o* . . .) You now have given your accomplice two letters, "l" and "o".

You go on. Next you think you'll visit Venice. (And there we have another place-name, a "V".)

You finish it off by saying you'll hang around Venice for at least two days. (Another number and another vowel: two days means the second vowel: a, *e* . . .)

You have given all four letters—love.

These are the basic bones, the key to remember. London, four, Venice, two.

But now let's assume that the group wants you to transmit the name of a famous person to your partner; for example, L. B. Johnson. You wouldn't spell out Johnson in your monologue. That's too obvious.

Try giving the name through a series of clues, simple words that are closely associated with the famous person. For Johnson, you might do *President, U. S. A.*

"I'm going from Paris (P) to Rome (R), stay at least two (E) weeks, and then on to Sicily (S) for I hope three (I) days before I head back to Dijon (D) where I have to stay two (E) nights before going on to Nice (N) and Torino (T).

"I haven't decided definitely, but next I think I must take a plane . . ."

This is very important. A mention of transportation indicates the end of a word and the beginning of a new one.

"I shall fly either to Uruguay (U) or Siam (S) for one (A) solid year."

You've done it. You've spelled out *President, U. S. A.*

If your accomplice is still in the dark—as well he might be with thirty-six presidents to choose from—he'll need another word. "Living" might give it to him, but even there he has a choice. Better try "current."

After you have rested you are going on to Cairo (C) for

five (U) months to study ancient history. You hope there'll be occasional trips down to Rosetta (R) to look at the stone and back to Rome (R) for another two (E) months at least, before you settle down again in either Naples (N) or Tripoli (T).

It may seem a peculiar trip, but your partner ought to have the words *President, U. S. A., current*—and with that in mind he should be able to think of Johnson.

PHONE CALL

The number of codes the human mind can devise is of course infinite, but occasionally you come across one that is very special. It may not always be the code itself, but the way it was first presented that enchants you. You know you've been had, but you'll never forget it.

This happened to me recently. When I arrived at a friend's house there was a deck of cards open on his desk. He asked me to choose one, which in itself was a little unusual, since he is not a game man. I remember I drew the two of hearts, but at this point, just as I was showing it to him his wife came into the room and told me there'd been a phone call before I arrived. "Oh yes," my friend said, "a Bob Andrews wants you to call," and he gave me his number.

I know no one by that name but my curiosity is such that even before we went on with the game I called the number and asked to speak with Bob Andrews.

The voice at the other end, a voice I did not recognize, told me that Mr. Andrews was not in, but he thought there was a message for me. I waited, and in a moment the voice went on. It was all quite mysterious. It seemed Mr. Andrews wanted me to know, the voice said, that the card I was holding was the two of hearts.

It was several hours before my friend would explain. The number I had called was the liquor store at the corner. He and the manager had worked out the simplest of all codes.

B (for Bob) the second letter of the alphabet meant a two, and A (for Andrews) meant it was a heart. The manager kept a list tacked up by the phone.

This has been elaborated upon since. Sometimes now the voice that answers says that Mr. B— A— or F— C—, whoever has been asked for, was murdered a few hours ago. He then adds that the police have only one clue, it seems the poor fellow was holding a certain playing card. . . .

Try it. Work out a deal with someone you know who will be staying around a phone all evening, or why not with your own friendly liquor store?

14:   *Your Own Originals*

THE MAN AT THE MAILBOX

On a cool, clear October night some years ago I was driving home from Culver City, heading north along Doheny Drive. A soft breeze came in from the sea, the top was back on the car and the radio was playing a medley of old Gershwin songs. I felt fine, my world seemed very good.

At the corner of Third I stopped for a light.

I cannot remember now what it was that made me aware of the little man on the corner. He was standing by a mailbox, a seemingly normal, middle-aged, well-dressed man. However there was something about him, something in his manner . . .

First, I noticed him take a pack of matches from his pocket and light one, but then, instead of putting it to the cigarette which was hanging from his lip, I watched him place the burning match against the other matches. They immediately shot up in a little flame and for a half moment more the man stood holding the small fire, then he carefully opened the mailbox and dropped the blazing matches inside. He waited still another moment, then turned and walked away down Third. The traffic light changed from red to green and . . . But why go on? That's the end of the story.

It's the end of the story, but it is the beginning of a question I've been asking myself—and anyone else who'd listen —for the past ten years.

What, under these circumstances—sitting in your car on a fine fall night and seeing this—what does one do?

I hope it bothers you as much as it does me.

Try it, after you've worried awhile yourself, on a few close friends. I think you will find their answers are, at least surprising.

Should you get out and grab the fellow? Should you call the police?

My grandfather, I have realized, would have had none of my qualms. With that clear black-and-white morality of an earlier generation there would have been no hesitation. "The fellow is mad. Furthermore he is trespassing and should be handed over to the authorities. And no delay!" (Yes sir, Grandpa.)

Fran, a friend of mine, feels that one should get out of the car, approach the poor man quietly, gently, try to establish "rapport" and somehow lead him not to the police, but to a good doctor. (Fran, need I add, has been in group therapy for six months now.)

Her husband, Jim, doesn't agree. "He's a nut, how are you going to reason with a nut? Drive on." (Jim is not in group.)

A great many you will find say, "Drive on."

In fact, in all these years I have discovered only one completely satisfactory answer. I met Christopher Isherwood once and was able to put the question to him. I must say there was not much hesitation here either. He said, "Well now, I should be very careful not to post a letter in that mailbox."*

The above may be used as an example of what game books call "conversation openers" or "icebreakers." Since starting this collection I have glanced at some of the more standard publications on the subject and for the most part they are splendid, well-written, scholarly books, but a great prepon-

---

* At dinner the other night Helen Wynn cut through all the nonsense and asked, "But what *did* you do?" and I had to tell her. I did nothing, because you see, I made it up.

Since writing this it has been brought to my attention that all manner of things are being put in mailboxes now. Army officers deposit kittens in them (see Carson McCullers' *Reflections in a Golden Eye*), babies are left there by small brothers (New York *Times*, July 1, 1963), etc., etc.

derance of them seems to be aimed at cruise directors or inhibited hostesses, people who look upon games as a form of "organized activity" with very special rules that must be studied and mastered before a group assembles.

To me games are an extremely individual habit. The way a man chooses to play one is as personal a matter as the way he shaves himself.

(Did you ever suggest to a mature male that the proper way to begin shaving is under the left sideburn? The next morning, I can promise you, he will start off right under his nose, shaving away exactly as he's been doing for years. And quite right he is.)

Perhaps because I feel so strongly about this, I am convinced that the best of all games are those we make up ourselves—and often when we are very young.

"A man's friends die, get drunk, or move out of town; but the questions, the things he is curious about as a youth, remain and will fascinate him always." I don't know who wrote that—I read it years ago—but whoever he was, he was speaking to my condition.

As a youth, I must admit, unlike more sensitive boys, I was not particularly concerned with the phenomena of nature, with what the wind might be saying, etc. If there was a secret murmuring to me deep in some conch shell, it was of passing interest. However, what I saw the grown-ups doing—and the reasons behind their doing it—fascinated me then and fascinates me still.

What follows here are my questions with a few notes about how they came into being. Some have been made up, some borrowed from other game addicts. A few have been adapted so that more than one player may join in (these appear with rules and suggestions for scoring). But most of them come under the heading of Lonely Pleasures— what to do while waiting for a bus, in a dentist's office, or when trapped at the Courthouse after being called for jury duty.

If the notes are unduly autobiographical, or if there seem too many references to Southern California, this cannot be helped. Seven years of my life were spent there and they were long years.

Shirley Booth said almost all that need be said about Hollywood: "No matter how hot it is during the day, there is nothing to do at night."

And while I'm name-dropping, just one more. When Elaine May—of Mike and Elaine—was asked about L.A., she told the interviewer, "I feel in opposition to almost everything anyway, but it comes to its height in Los Angeles."

I have never met Miss May, but oh, how I understand that girl.

EVERY MAN HAS HIS PRICE

This is exactly what the title implies and the object of the game is to discover what some of our prices are.

Start by asking a fairly simple one: Would you sell, or let us cut off, two of the toes on your left foot for five thousand dollars? A great many people—and this may surprise you—will say no. Go on to ten thousand, fifteen . . .

My friend George Bradshaw will let you go as high as you like, but around twenty thousand I can see Katherine Eunson beginning to consider. And certainly at twenty-five thousand a deal can be arranged.*

If you get nowhere in the anatomy line, shift to morals (is that the word?). Would you consider an affair with ——————— (name a really unattractive tycoon) for, let us say, ——————— (suggest a staggering sum).

If the answer is still no, start making conditions. If this brief affair would guarantee your family absolute security, would you change your mind?

* A letter arrived from Katherine this week. "I have never felt the same about Bradshaw. What good are toes? They were his toes he said and he wanted them. But think of all that money, tax free, think what he could have done with it. . . ."

You may find some melting here.

If your baby were dying and your only way to get the life-saving serum flown in to the child depended on this affair . . . would you then?

The melodramatic heart is touched, answers change.

INVENTORY

You are waiting for a bus. You know there is nothing you can do. You might light a cigarette. Some say this works. Immediately after the cigarette is lit a bus will appear. This is not so for me.

Buses are cowards. They will not go out alone. (I should not speak for Cleveland or South Boston, but about the L.A. and N.Y.C. transportation systems I am an authority.) Sometimes they may wait and venture forth in pairs, but on the Lexington Avenue line they move only in coveys, and the one suggestion I have for coping is to try to accept the reality of how small, how unimportant we are compared to a bus and then try to concentrate on an Inventory.

Inventories should be taken of shopwindows that are located not too far from the bus stop. The point of the game is to select an object—and you must select one—that you will take back and live with in your one-room apartment. (I don't care who you are, for this game you live in one room.)

The selection is particularly taxing if you change buses near an auction gallery. There is one where I wait whose windows are jam-packed with objets d'art which I can only believe came out of the old Roxy, or possibly the grand salon of a brothel in Saratoga Springs: Chinese vases eight feet high, great gilt throne chairs, endless rows of life-sized marble ladies pouring marble water onto marble flowers.

One object, remember, to live with in one room.

Of course, the neighborhood that you wait in colors the game. I know a young secretary who changes every evening at Fifth Avenue and Fifty-seventh Street, in front of Tiffany's. Her problem is rather special.

THE NEXT ONE YOU MEET

I can't remember where or when I played this game for the first time, but I remember all too vividly where I played it last: the Seventy-second Street entrance to Central Park.

It is primarily a game for city walkers and especially city dog-walkers, those who go out early in the morning or early in the evening when the streets are not quite deserted. Immediately before or after the rush hour is best.

The trick is to study the people walking toward you, but this time you study them in a rather special way, from the point of view of marriage. (If the idea of marriage to anyone is frightening, you may want to change it to a month in a cabin in Maine.)

Most men will eliminate the first woman who heads in their direction and the second. (I'm fairly certain the appraisal of men by women follows this same line.)

You'll probably let the third and fourth go by too, but at

seven and eight—careful. Because you have only two more chances. If you have not accepted one before number ten, you are stuck permanently with number ten.

One inevitable sideline of the game you'll find is that at some point you will begin to wonder how many of those passing may be playing the same game about you.

It was that thought plus the notion of being permanently stuck with a number ten that made me give up the game.

One winter morning I was walking my dog across Seventy-second. It was early, with what I considered a comfortable number on the street—no more than one or two women per block. I must have been feeling extremely lucky that day because I remember eliminating a very possible number nine as I crossed Fifth Avenue. Then, as I started down into the Park, it happened. Suddenly I was face to face with an old friend.

I mean old. She is a woman I've admired for years, but she will not see seventy again.

I had never known her well, but I often saw her striding through the park. We were in the habit of stopping and chatting about the weather, our dogs, mutual friends, but this morning I could not speak. I stammered. I blushed like a young Holden Caulfield, and then hurried away.

It had something to do with the picture of a cabin in Maine.

MIS-INFORMATION

This is ideal for those who like to get to the theater early, yet find waiting a bore, or for those few who stay in their seats at intermission.

Turn to your partner and in a conversational tone, but still with enough voice to be heard by the person behind you, ask if she didn't love Julie Harris in *My Fair Lady*.

This may get no immediate response, so broaden your

approach. Admit how delighted you were when Julie won her Oscar for *The Miracle Worker*.

It's only a question of time—and often a very short time. The one behind you will lean forward, smile, and correct you. You mean Julie Andrews. And it was Anne Bancroft in *The Miracle Worker*.

You can cover any number of subjects and it can be played in any number of places—the ballet, the opera, ball parks.

Watch it around election time, though. It is not called Mis-information then; it is the kind of dirty lies Republicans are always spreading about Democrats, or vice versa.

MIS-MATING

In the early days of the present administration there was a small news item in the Washington papers which apparently made a much deeper impression on me than I'd realized at the time.

One of the new young administrators and his bride were planning a large gala, but when they sent their social secretary—who I can only assume was equally new at her job—to pick up the guest list from a file in his office, she picked up the wrong file box. Later that evening she was discovered busily addressing invitations not to a group of dignitaries, but to a list of underworld thugs the young administrator had recently been investigating.

The possibilities implicit here, the thoughts of what might have occurred, won't let me rest. In fact, I have become extremely fond of this secretary and can picture all sorts of parties she might arrange.

We may imagine, for the sake of a game, that she is as uninformed about the leaders of our "cultural boom" as she is of the leaders of the underworld. Think then of the groups she might assemble.

Or let's say she works only from the last names she finds

in her files. Proceeding along this line, here are a few she might invite in for dinner believing that they were couples:

Bertrand and Roz Russell
Tennessee and Esther Williams
Maxwell and Liz Taylor
Ramsay and Jeanette MacDonald

You can use your friends, of course. There's a character actress I'm extremely fond of, Elizabeth Patterson. I am delighted about an invitation going out to

Floyd and Elizabeth Patterson

But make your own list, it's going to be quite an evening.

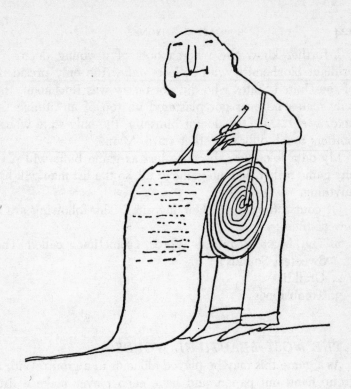

15: List Collectors

There is a great similarity between game-players and list-makers, and to the best of my knowledge no psychiatrist has discovered exactly what the connection is, but I may have some helpful data for them. (In fact, if a foundation ever considers earmarking a few thousand for such a study, I'd like them to know I am available.)

Among my papers I have the address of a most successful screenwriter who lists his *nevers*, all the simple, ordinary things he has never done: he has never slept in a tent, he has never owned a pair of two-toned sport shoes, etc.

I further know the whereabouts of a young doctor, a brilliant biochemist, who collects *onlys:* the only president of the United States who did not marry was Buchanan, the only man who ever got plastered on top of an atomic reactor was L. M. (the doctor himself), the only state whose borders touch only one other state—Maine.

My data is endless, because just as game buffs will play any game rather than no game at all, so the list man will list anything.

Of course they have their favorites. The following are a few of them:

1. The Most Beautiful Words (sometimes called The Sweetest Sounds)
2. Graffiti
3. Tombstones

THE MOST BEAUTIFUL WORDS

As a game this may be played alone or in a group. With a group hand out papers and have each player make a list, then read them aloud and guess, as in Revelations.

The answers indeed may be revelations. The word "doctor" turned up the other night at the top of a list and "mother" and "father" often appear. That *must* mean something.

Your list may be as silly or as sensible, as sacred or as profane as your mood dictates.

The first reference I've found to a list of the Most Beautiful Words was one compiled by Mr. Wilfred Funk:*

dawn
hush
lullaby
murmuring
tranquil
mist

* Certainly any lover of beauty who spread that name around must have felt obliged to make some kind of amends.

luminous
chimes
gold
melody

Funk's famous ten which appeared in the early Thirties were apparently the cue for all manner of folk to start offering up their own. Rupert Hughes suggested:

immemorial
oriole
threnody
tremulous
blithe
translucent
ivory
gloom
inviolate
blue

Miss Jane Addams, who it is surprising to realize was here among us and reading her newspaper just thirty years ago, answered in a characteristic way with one word:

neighbor

With this we seem to be getting nearer to the meaning of a word and not only its sound. This must have been what Rolf Hoffman had in mind when he suggested a combination of words he'd found in a Sandburg poem:

the synthesis of hyacinths
and biscuits.

But I have no idea what Edwin Markham was aiming for when he submitted, among others:

reverberate
chryselephantine
empyrean
imperishable
ideal
California

One would have thought Dorothy Parker would have put an end to the game when—sensible woman—she said that to her the most beautiful words in the language are:
check enclosed

Ring Lardner offered his list too:
gangrene
flit
scram
mange
wretch
smoot
guzzle
McNoboe
blute
crene

Later Mr. Lardner explained that blute was "a smoker who doesn't inhale," and crene was "a man who inhales but doesn't smoke."

DEFINITIONS

One outgrowth of the lists of the thirties may be definitions. This can be played several ways. Sylvia Bigelow has great success just opening the dictionary, finding a large, unfamiliar word and tossing it out for each player to define. She gets some amazing results. But I prefer choosing important, five-dollar words such as U.S.A., God, or Poetry.

With God you are on your own, but after defining U.S.A., I suggest you try reading aloud what some others have said, for example, the opening passage of Dos Passos' *U.S.A.*, which you remember is a series of definitions. Here are a few:

U.S.A. is the slice of a continent.

U.S.A. is a group of holding companies, some aggregations of trade unions, a set of laws bound in calf . . .

a set of stock quotations rubbed out and written in by a Western Union boy on a blackboard . . .

a public library full of old newspapers and dog-eared history books with protests scrawled on the margins in pencil.

U.S.A. is the world's greatest river-valley fringed with mountains and hills.

U.S.A. is a set of big mouthed officials with too many bank accounts.

U.S.A. is a lot of men buried in their uniforms in Arlington Cemetery.

U.S.A. is the letters at the end of an address when you're away from home.

But mostly U.S.A. is the speech of the people.

After you've tried defining poetry, take a look at what the poets have to say. Two of my favorites are, Sandburg's:

Poetry is the journal of a sea animal living on land, wanting to fly the air.

Poetry is a search for syllables to shoot at the barriers of the unknown and the unknowable.

Poetry is a theorem of a yellow-silk handkerchief knotted with riddles, sealed in a balloon tied to the tail of a kite flying in a white wind against a blue sky in spring.

Poetry is a phantom script telling how rainbows are made and why they go away.

Poetry is the opening and closing of a door, leaving those who look through to guess about what is seen during a moment.

And one by John Holmes:

Poetry is what you thought about when you were a child, somehow not forgotten in the business of growing up, and discovered to be true, and valuable, and possible, just as you always thought it was.

MOST RECOGNIZABLE CHARACTER

There's one personal little list I'd like to sneak in here.

The first time I met Miriam Howell she asked me a question: "What characters in fiction do you feel you know so well that you would not be surprised by anything they did or said, if they walked into the room?"

I thought about it and made my list, then one of those uncanny things happened. The top three on my list were the top three on hers.

I don't see Miriam very much now, but I'll always feel a bond. We know the same people.

You may want to add this to the questions in *Revelations* (page 32), but it is also one to do alone. I find it quite helpful in the dentist chair.

P.S.: At the top of our lists (and this dates us both) were Jay Gatsby, Soames Forsyte, and Eugene Gant. In the past few years I have had to add only one name to this group, and I have a feeling he might appear on a great many other lists, Holden Caulfield.

GRAFFITI

I have no intention of adding to the Kilroy mystery. It is undoubtedly the most famous bit of Graffiti of modern times, and like every American who had any connection with World War II, everywhere I went I found the words "Kilroy was here." Others may worry about its origins, who Kilroy was in the first place, its international implications, and how it possibly could have been scribbled out in certain spots before our troops arrived.

I mention it only because as an example of Graffiti it is (a) printable and (b) it marks the beginning of my getting hooked, the first step in my becoming a Graffiti collector.

In the African theater—which is the only one I can speak

of—there was another phrase that almost equaled Kilroy. I saw it in latrines, on the sides of ambulances, on doors of transport planes from Cairo to Casablanca. And for sheer ambiguity it stays at the top of my list:

What do you want—egg in your beer?

Until then I had assumed that anything scrawled on a public wall would be, if not scatological, at least too dull to bother with. I knew, of course, that anthropologists derived a certain bang out of discovering scorecards and funny sayings inscribed on the walls at Herculaneum, possibly dating back to 100 B.C. But for our times I was sure it was a lost art. Then, shortly after Kilroy and "egg in your beer" at the close of the war, I worked for a year in Washington, D. C. And it was there in the men's room of the old O.P.A. Building that I made my first real "find." Someone had written in pencil, and I quote exactly—

T. S. Elliot loves D. H. Lawrence

and above this, with a great arrow pointing to it, someone else had added in ink—

Eliot is spelled with one l,
you ass.

From that day on I have been a Graffiti man.

Unfortunately—and as it has turned out quite embarrassingly—on almost this same day my doctor discovered that I badly needed to wear glasses for reading. I don't care to go into detail now, it is not at all comfortable to remember a few occasions when friends have come upon me putting on a pair of spectacles to read the fine print scribbled on subway posters. However, the chance for a "find" has been irresistible, and several I've come across have been worth any chagrin.

One other thing that has helped has been the knowledge that I was not alone. In fact, a certain prestige was added to the movement one spring when "finds" began turning up in the *Herald Tribune* book section.

One of these certainly belongs as a mate of my T. S. Eliot. It was found in a phone booth in the Times Square area, and it states clearly and emphatically—

Schopenhauer is a fink.

Later in this same spring Edward Albee let it be known in an interview that he'd first seen his famous phrase "Who's Afraid of Virginia Woolf" scribbled on a coffeehouse wall.

But the greatest of all to me is one sent in to the *Trib* by a Miss Letty Cotten who found it written "in a neat hand in the Providence, Rhode Island, bus station . . ."

Children
Lost in a haunted wood
Who
Have never been happy or good.

Whose neat hand wrote that? And why?

If any of the above speaks to you and you think you might become a Graffiti hunter, I should warn you, you will soon be faced with a moral question. You will want to write back. Some of the questions demand answers.

So far I have resisted, I have not defiled the walls of any public building, but will this go on?

The temptation was almost too great one afternoon on the fourth floor of the New York State Supreme Court Building.

As far as I could make out, an argument had been started with the simple statement:

Peace is the most!

To this someone with another colored chalk had added:

Ban the Bomb.

Several angry arrows pointed to this with a great many four letter words and the inevitable accusations and epithets about Communism. Then still farther out, but still joined in by an arrow-like line was:

What the hell, if the bomb
falls you'll all get killed.

And right next to this a happier type suggested:

So! Live today.

This still was not the end. In a heavy, dark blue ink someone else asked:

What are you doing about
the Bomb, bud?

It was all I could do not to take out my pencil and bring
it to some conclusion. I resisted. But each morning I found
I had to make my way up to the fourth floor to see what had
been added.

My term of jury duty finally ended and I haven't been
back to the Courthouse. I often wonder if the debate is still
raging. I hope so.

At Christmastime in Greenwich Village I came across
what I believe is my all-time favorite. Again it was in a wash-
room, printed on the wall in clear block letters:

A merry Christmas to all
our readers.

TOMBSTONES

Tracking down strange epitaphs differs in some respects
from hunting for Graffiti, but together I'm sure they represent

the oldest game in this collection, if not in all of history. We know ancient man did not accomplish much before he started making comments about it on the sides of tombs—and the moment the words were written out, there must have been those who had to go over and take a look.

Perhaps the best way to show what it is that can still pull so many of us off the throughways in search of New England churchyards, or a Victorian cemetery hidden in the center of a business district, is to list several prize "finds."*

Of the hundreds I have to choose from, not many delight me more than the simple inscription which stands over the family plot of Robert R. Hallenbeck in Elgin, Minnesota. It states:

> None of us ever voted for
> Roosevelt or Truman

But Republicans aren't the only ones to want their convictions known. In the Old Burying Ground at Marcellus, New York, the stone of Julia, wife of Thos. Andrews, reads:

> I recommended religion to all.

Dear woman, straight to the point. And out in Pekin, Indiana, there is one dated 1865:

> He believed nothing but the
> success of the Democratic
> Party could ever save this
> Union

It may be what the students of Zen call an "awareness of something ancestral in ourselves" that draws many of us into old graveyards. That, or a kind of hopeful curiosity. There is

---

* Again, some of these are my own discoveries, some have been sent by friends from their collections. Special reference should be made to Charles L. Wallis' brilliant book, *Stories on Stone* (New York: Oxford University Press, 1954). And my special thanks to Martha C. Parsons of Baltimore for allowing me the use of her private collection.

always the wondrous chance that as we search through the
tangled underbrush we may stumble (literally) upon a forgotten piece of our history, or come face to face with one of
those unfinished, and unfinishable, stories.

Certainly there are few people around now I'd rather put
a couple of questions to than a Miss Ivy Saunders of Shutes-
bury, Massachusetts, who erected this stone:

> To the four husbands
> of Miss Ivy Saunders
> 1790, 1794, 1808, 18—
> Here lies my husbands one, two, three
> Dumb as men could ever be
> As for my fourth, well praise be God
> He bides for a little above the sod.
>
> Alex, Ben, Sandy
> Were the first three names
> And to make things tidy
> I'll add his name—James.

I'd also like to know a little more about Cynthia and
Steven, buried in Hollis, New Hampshire, 1780:

> Here lies Cynthia, Steven's wife
> She lived six years in calm and strife
> Death came at last to set her free
> I was glad and so was she

And poor Mrs. Job Brooks of Concord, Massachusetts,
1786:

> Lived with her husband upwards
> of sixty five years, she died in
> the hope of resurrection to a
> better life.

But certainly the most intriguing of all "unfinished" stories
is one in Little Compton, Rhode Island:

> In Memory of Elizabeth who
> should have been the wife
> of Mr. Simeon Palmer who died
> August 14th 1776 in the 64th
> Year of her age.

Why? In whose opinion should she have been his wife? This is the sort of question that can keep us searching through hundreds of duller inscriptions.

I have a real respect for the frankness of this one up in Lincoln, Maine:

> 1800
>
> Sacred to the Memory of Jared Bates
>
> His widow aged 24, living at 7 Elm
> Street has every qualification
> for a good wife and yearns to be
> comforted.

Of course all don't present questions. There are those with which I feel instant identification, as I did with this one I ran across one gloomy afternoon in Greenmount Cemetery, Baltimore. There was no name that I could make out, no clear date, but I know the man:

> He meant well
> He tried often
> He failed much.

I also have a certain feeling for this fellow buried up in Providence, Rhode Island:

> 1803–1823
> The wedding day decided was
> The wedding wine provided
> But ere the day did come along
> He drank it up and died did
>   O Sidney! Sidney!

And there is not much question about the sort of girl Arabella was:

> Hatfield, Mass.—
> Beaneath this stone,
> A lump of clay
> Lies Arabella Young
> Who on the 21st of May
> 177— (?)
> Began to hold her tongue.

In fact, I think my favorites are those that tell a full story, give all the pertinent details, and often in the fewest possible words, yet still manage to point out a warning.

As children my brothers and I were driven down into southern Maryland to look at the grave of poor Peter Baker in Smallwood:

> Here lies our Son dead,
> Someone hit him on the
> head.

There's not much more I need to know about Peter. And the same goes for Mrs. Smets, buried in Skaneateles, New York:

> Neuralgia worked on Mrs. Smets
> Till neath the sod it laid her
> She was a worthy Methodist
> And served as a crusader

In Gerard, Pennsylvania, Ellen Shannon speaks for herself:

> In memory of
> Ellen Shannon
> Aged 26 years
> Who was fatally burned
> March 21st 1870
> by the explosion of a lamp

filled with "R. E. Danforth's
Non explosive
Burning fluid"

Sometimes it is impossible not to wonder about the rhymes.
Were these facts accurate, or did the jokers in Sargentville,
Maine, find this couplet irresistible?

In memory of Mr. Peter Daniels

Born Aug. 7, 1688, dyed May 20, 1746

Beneath this stone a lump of clay
Lies Uncle Peter Daniels
Who too early in the month of May
Took off his winter flannels

Also if you're considering taking this up as a hobby, at
some point you'll probably begin to worry about plagiarism
in the churchyard. This bothered me considerably in Old St.
Paul's in New York where all the "lovely babes" were told:

. . . take thy rest
because He thought it best.

And when from various mishaps folks *were slain* they all
knew that "in Him they'd rise *again*." Later it was pointed
out to me that if these had not been suggested by the same
stonecutter or clergyman, they were probably lifted from one
of the pamphlets which were so popular in colonial days and
always contained along with helpful hints "your choice of
five hundred original inscriptions to commemorate the dead."

Then, too, how many rhymes can you think up for a grave?
What else rhymes with forgotten? I trust this was their problem in Milford, Connecticut, when Martha Fowler died in
the year 1792:

Molly tho pleasant in her day
Was suddenly seized and sent away
How soon she's ripe. How soon she's rotten
Sent to her grave and soon forgotten.

Perhaps it was this same need for a rhyme pattern that dictated the sentiment on Sarah Shute's stone in Canaan, New Hampshire:

> Sarah Shute
> 1803–1840
> Here lies cutdown like unripe fruit
> The wife of deacon Amos Shute
> She died of drinking too much coffee
> Anno domini eighteen forty

There are two more warnings on my list. One is from Burlington, Massachusetts:

> 1796
> Here lies the body of Susan Lowder
> Who burst while drinking sedlitz powder
> Called from this world to her heavenly
> rest
> She should have waited 'till it effervessed

The other was sent to me by a friend, who had been sent it by a friend who had found it in Wales. (You see how this can get you?)

> Here I lie with my 4 daughters
> Dead of drinking cheltenham water
> If we'd only stuck to Epson salts
> We wouldn't be lying in these here vaults

In 1927 *Vanity Fair* asked a group of celebrities to write their own epitaphs. It may have seemed a ghoulish joke at the time, but if you think about it, the precedent for this goes back to ancient Egypt. Most great poets—Burns, Gray, Coleridge, Pope—have all tried their hand at it.

Perhaps the most famous early American attempt is Ben Franklin's:

The Body of BENJAMIN FRANKLIN,
Printer,
Like the Covering of an old Book,
Its Contents torn out,
And stript of its Lettering and Gilding,
Lies here, Food for Worms;

But the Work shall not be lost,
It will (as he believed) appear once more,
In a new and more beautiful Edition,
Corrected and amended
By the Author.

Few of the 1927 celebrities equaled Franklin, but among the group there was one by Mr. W. C. Fields that is my all time favorite. I'd like to end with this.

W. C. FIELDS
I'd rather be in Philadelphia

Index